Glory Days

American Musclecars
1964–1973

The Complete Street Machine Library™

Glory Days

American Musclecars *1964–1973*

National Street Machine Club
Minnetonka, Minnesota

Glory Days
American Musclecars 1964–1973

Printed in 2008.

Published by the National Street Machine Club under license from MBI Publishing Company.

Tom Carpenter
Creative Director

Heather Koshiol
Managing Editor

Jen Weaverling
Production Editor

Teresa Marrone
Book Design and Production

4 5 6 7 8 9 10 / 12 11 10 09 08
ISBN: 978-1-58159-308-2
© Robert Genat, 1999, 2006
© Bill Holder, 2002, 2006
© Phil Kunz, 2002, 2006
© Dan Lyons, 2001, 2006
© David Newhardt, 2001, 2006
© Jason Scott, 2001, 2006

National Street Machine Club
12301 Whitewater Drive
Minnetonka, MN 55343
www.streetmachineclub.com

About the Authors/Photographers

Robert Genat *is an award winning author and photographer who has written over two dozen books. A self-proclaimed "gearhead," Robert has restored several musclecars and currently drives a chopped deuce coupe on a daily basis. He and his wife, Robin, own and operate Zone Five Photo in Encinitas, California.*

Bill Holder *is a retired aero engineer now working as an automotive and aerospace writer. His work has appeared in numerous automotive magazines, such as* Open Wheel, Super Chevy, Muscle Car Review, *and* AutoWeek.

Photographer **Phil Kunz** *specializes in high-speed action motorsports photography of automobiles and hydroplanes. His photographs have appeared in at least 25 different automotive and powerboat magazines. Kunz lives in the Dayton, Ohio, area.*

Dan Lyons *is a frequent contributor to* Collectible Automobile *and* Automobile Quarterly, *among others. A member of the International Motor Press Association and the Motor Press Guild, Lyons resides in Latham, New York.*

David Newhardt *is one of the best automobile photographers working today and has provided photography for best-selling titles* Corvette Fifty Years *and* Mustang Forty Years. *He resides in Pasadena, California.*

Jason Scott *has more than 20 years' experience overhauling musclecars of all makes and models for hundreds of articles that have appeared in numerous automotive magazines. He lives in Saco, Maine, with his wife, Michelle, and two children, Jenna and Cameron. Scott's other books include:* Camaro Restoration Guide: 1967-1969; Camaro Z-28 and Performance Specials; Original Camaro 1967-1969; *and* How to Tune & Modify Your Camaro, 1982-1998.

On the front cover (from top to bottom):
1971 GSX, pages 20–21; 1969 BOS 302, pages 100–101; 1970 Plymouth Superbird, pages 152–153; and 1970 Pontiac Judge ("The Judge"), page 63.

CONTENTS

Introduction

For cars and car lovers, they truly were the *Glory Days* — from the viewpoints of both performance and style.

The mid-1960s through the early 1970s generated automobiles like those that had never been seen before ... and will never be produced again. It was almost like the factories were turning our purebred racecars and selling them from dealership showrooms!

And the cars became legends: essential icons of American culture, both then and now.

These awesome vehicles earned the name "musclecars" for a couple reasons — the performance they offered, and the style they showed. Incredible "muscle power" could be found under their hoods — massive amounts of horsepower generated by huge cubic inch counts, big compression ratios, and oversized (or in some cases multiple) carburetors. And the cars just looked tough — with light, handsome, streamlined bodies that produced good suspension and allowed for breathless performance.

Maybe most amazing of all, the "big three" automakers competed hotly to see who could create the best, and sell the most, of these high-powered products.

During these musclecar wars, General Motors girded for battle and created some confirmed classics. The competition cowered at the mere mention of all the models from GM's Buick, Chevrolet, Oldsmobile and Pontiac lines.

By 1965, Ford's Mustang was blazing down America's streets and setting sales records along the way. Recognized as the first pony car, Fords' high-powered but nimble-handling sports coupe actually sparked the musclecar revolution into existence.

Not to be outdone, Chrsyler may have well outdone them all with its Hemi-powered creations. When it comes to big-block musclecar performance, the Hemi set the standard ... a standard that we still look to with awe and admiration to this day.

So come along on a wonderful journey through the *Glory Days* of America's musclecars as we track their evolution from their not-so-humble beginning through the mid 1970's. It was a time to remember, it is still a time to savor ... and it did indeed produce some glorious rides!

Because the look of the 1966 GTO was so successful, few changes were made in the 1967 GTO's appearance. The parking lights were still located in the grille openings, but the texture of the grille was of a wider pattern.

The Boss 429 is one of the best and one of the most exclusive big-block Mustangs ever built. The Big Boss was a Mustang SportsRoof with a racing engine crammed into the tight confines of the engine bay. The 429 was created so Ford would comply with the minimum build rules of NASCAR stock racing. Although the 429 was a competent musclecar, it didn't realize its full potential in stock form due to a mild cam and a small carburetor, but when its engine was fitted with an aggressive cam, a larger carburetor, and large headers, it was more than a match for most musclecars.

The gas cap clearly identifies its maker, Carroll Shelby. This is a Shelby GT350H. For a nominal fee, one could rent a supercar in the mid 1960s and this particular one was fitted with a high-output 289 small block and an automatic transmission.

The 1960 Corvette was a great example of late-'50s-era styling. From its two-tone paint, to the toothy chrome grille, it was a flashy American sports car that symbolized the time. The optional fuel-injected 283-ci V-8 engine had plenty of power to back up the look. 1960 marked the first year for both front and rear anti-sway bars under the Corvette, and the last year for the legendary grillework. Note the wide white-wall tires, which were more typical on full-size cars, but look at home on this year Corvette.

Chapter One

GM Muscle

It was a shining-star time period from a performance point of view, an era that will live forever in automotive history. The mid-1960s through the early 1970s brought forth performance and styling that had never been seen before. It was as if the factories were turning out purebred race cars and selling them from dealership showrooms. These cars were called "Musclecars."

The amazing aspect of this phenomenon was the fact that the Big Three, and even American Motors, were all competing to sell these high-powered products. The horsepower, for the most part, was generated by big cubic inches, big compression ratios, and big carburetors or, in some cases, multiple carbs. The power figures quoted for the big-block powerplants of the era were startling, in a number of cases exceeding 400 horsepower. Add a light body plus suitable suspension, and breathless performance was inevitable.

For Pontiac, the GTO epitomized performance and power. The first version came in 1964 and featured a triple-carbed 389-ci powerplant. This particular GTO is a 1968 version, with a 400-ci powerplant under the hood. Pontiac also offered muscle Firebirds and Trans Ams with outstanding performance capabilities.

Buick surprised everyone when it decided to build musclecars. This '70 GS Stage 1 was one of the top Buick performance machines.

Almost all of the divisions in the large companies were involved with this chase, including the Plymouth and Dodge divisions of Chrysler; the Ford and Mercury divisions of Ford; and the Buick, Chevrolet, Oldsmobile, and Pontiac divisions of General Motors (GM). Each division had its unique performance engines, and each model and brand had its own cult of devoted buying fans.

Buick was possibly the most surprising GM division to delve into the muscle phenomenon. Normally associated with prestige models, Buick didn't have a performance image, but that certainly changed during this period. Buick's Gran Sport, Stage 1, and GSX models were as quick, or quicker, than most of the competition. The division's top powerplant was a 455-ci Stage 1 mill capable of 360 announced horsepower. In reality, the engine produced much more!

Then came the Chevy line, which included five models with muscle connotations: Chevelle, Nova, Corvette, Camaro, and Monte Carlo.

The Vette in the 1950s used muscular versions of the 327-ci engine. In the 1960s, both the Vette and Camaro were first fitted with powerful 350-ci engines before moving to big-block powerplants. The top Vette engine would be the awesome 427, while the Camaro's largest powerplant would be a 396-ci engine, although certain special models also carried a 427-ci mill. The largest engine for the Nova would be a 402. The Chevelle was fitted with both the potent 396-ci and 454-ci engines. A 454 was also the biggest engine for the Monte Carlo.

Oldsmobile accomplished similar success with its performance 442 model, which could be purchased with a number of bullish powerplants. The 442 was fitted with a number of different engines, up to a 455 with 365 horsepower.

The Chevy division offered muscular engines in its Chevelle, Nova, Corvette, Camaro, and Monte Carlo models. This 417 Chevrolet Office Production Order (COPO) Camaro was a low-production model rated at 425 horsepower.

Several Oldsmobile musclecars of the late 1960s and early 1970s featured legendary performance capabilities, including the 442, the W-30/31/32 series, and the Hurst models. Shown is a '70 442 W-30.

There were a number of performance "W" modifications to the Olds musclecars, including the W-30, W-31, and W-32 versions, with featured upgraded looks and powerplant performance tweaks. The top engine was the W-30 with 370 horses. Also, there were the Hurst Olds models that emphasized an external performance look, and the engines under their hoods matched that impression.

Pontiac had long been associated with motorsports and high performance, so its entry into the musclecar fray was easy and expected. Its performance image was established earlier with the heavy Grand Prix models of the early 1960s. With multi-carbed 428 powerplants, the Grand Prix models were killer machines!

But for most, the Pontiac musclecar image was initiated with the GTO family, first introduced in 1964 with the vaunted triple-carb powerplant. The engine size would continue to grow to 455 cubic inches during its heyday. There was also a flashy version of the GTO called "The Judge" that attracted a ton of attention. The Judge had the same engine as the GTO, but this version was a looker!

In 1967, Pontiac added another star to its musclecar galaxy with the potent Firebird/Trans Am family. A sporty model with genes that tied it to the Chevy Camaro, the model introduced big-time power to the

sports-car set. Performance was definitely the name of the game with a family of Ram-Air 400-cubic-inch engines, followed by even more powerful 455-ci engines.

The most powerful version of the 455-ci engine was the so-called 455 Super Duty that was out-and-out a pure racing engine. The Super Duty remains one of the most desired collectable muscle engines to this day.

What a performance era it was, and GM was right at the forefront.

Buick Transforms Its Image

Considered straight-laced and conservative, Buick cars were normally thought of as heavy four-door monsters. In the mid-1960s, it was an image that Buick was trying to shake. A Buick may very well be the family car that you grew up with. A Buick represented solidarity, and in the minds of some, it was an indication of a person's success in business. Buick projected all those images, but one image it still didn't have was that of a musclecar. No way! All that would soon change with the advent of the Gran Sport and the follow-up Stage 1 and GSX models. It was an amazing transformation.

This '71 Gran Sport shows its style from this front view. Note the horizontal stripes over the blacked-out grille and the red-lettered GS on the left side. The macho five-spoke wheels also gave the GS a look of high performance, opposed to the luxury look that Buick had been associated with for so long.

The Gran Sport (GS)

With the GS model, which was introduced in 1965 and lasted through the 1972 model year, Buick created an authentic musclecar and developed its unique muscle reputation. Not unlike many other GM muscle models of the period, the GS began life as an option of another model, the established Skylark. The GS option came along mid-1965 and included both performance and appearance aspects.

Included in the package was, most importantly, a brutish 401-ci powerplant rated at 325 horsepower at 4400 rpm. Actually, the corporate rule at the time was that there wasn't to be any displacement above 400, but somehow the GS's 401 slipped through. In addition to its impressive power, the 401 put out 445 pounds-feet of torque. A Carter AFB provided the fuel management with the compression ratio at 10:1, which was high for the time period. For the real performance-oriented, there was even a dealer-installed dual four-barrel carburetor option. On the GS models, the stock Skylark body was given a performance edge with red GS emblems on the roof quarters, deck, and grille.

A number of flashy appearance options on the '66 GS made it look a lot more like a musclecar. The hood ornament was deleted, but fake air scoops, a blacked-out grille, and side striping were added. The GS was maturing fast, but it was still not a model on its own.

The 1966 GS was fitted with basically the same 401 engine, which was officially known as the Wildcat 455. There's an interesting story on the nomenclature of the engine and the reason why there was a discrepancy of 54 between the two numbers. Normally, companies at the time liked to flaunt the number of cubic inches in the naming of their engines; in the case of the 401 engine, its torque rating (increased 10 to 455 pounds-feet for 1966) was more impressive than its displacement, so the engine was named Wildcat 455, rather than Wildcat 401.

For 1967, two versions of the GS were offered. The NR-coded 401 engine remained, although the horsepower rating was given a 15-horse boost to 340 and the model was dubbed "Skylark GS400." The GS400 featured a pair of hood scoops, a new grille design, and striping. The GS nametag was also tagged to a lower-powered version, the GS340, which carried a 340-ci, 260-horsepower (NR-coded) powerplant. It was a pretty impressive performance from a small block! Significant changes were made to the 400 engine, including larger intake and exhaust valves for better flow. Exhaust flow was further increased by the 400's larger manifolds. To effectively apply those horses to the ground, several rear-end gear ratios were offered. With manual transmissions, a 3.55:1 rear end was available unless air conditioning was also ordered. On special order, 3.90:1 or 4.30:1 positraction gears were also available. This was definitely not the Buick of the past!

As a low-production option, the GS340 was available in only two colors: silver or white. The GS340 was obviously aimed at those who weren't quite ready to pay for big-block performance. This more-streetable model received significant raves. Unfortunately, it was discontinued at the end of the model year.

It's interesting that the corporate advertising for the 1967 GS included all the expected Buick words such as big, roomy, and comfortable; however, it also included another surprising word that was most applicable: muscular.

For the 1968 model year, the GS became a model on its own and used the brand-new B body as its base. All the 1968 GS models took on performance looks for this model year with simulated air scoops on the fenders and a lower-body accent stripe. On the GS400, the classy-looking hood scoops were functional. Increased spring rates improved handling.

For 1968, the small-block GS model was the GS350, named for its new 350-ci, 280-horse-power engine. The GS400 was also back, in hardtop and convertible versions. The 350's extra

power was a result of its larger intake and exhaust manifolds from the 430-ci powerplant (the change was made for emission reasons), rather than the 10 ci of added displacement. The new 350 worked so well, it was carried over through the next two years of GS production. The most popular GS was the GS400 hardtop, with 10,743 sold. Next was the GS350, with 8,317 sold. GS400 convertibles were the rarest of the breed, as they still are today, with only 2,454 sold.

Induction was a new key word for the 1969 model year. The twin hood-mounted scoops on the GS400 fed cool air to the engine through a special twin-snorkel air cleaner. Although an official power increase was not announced, the scoops increased engine appreciability.

The RR-coded 400-ci engine carried a 340 horsepower rating, made at 5,000 rpm, while the RP-coded 350-ci engine could provide an impressive 280 horses. There was also a change in the carburetor, the former Carter AFB was deleted in favor of a 750-cfm Rochester four-barrel. Powered by the 400-ci engine, the 1969 GS was capable of quarter-mile times in the mid-14-second

For 1969, the GS was offered with a pair of punchy mills: A 400-ci engine producing 340 horsepower at 5000 rpm and the 350-ci engine shown here, which was capable of 280 horses. Even though the 350 had fewer cubes, it was still capable of impressive performance.

The design of the '69 GS was sweeping and stylish. A body crease stretched from the top of the front quarter and curved down to the front of the rear wheel opening. Front-end details included twin headlights and a horizontal bar across the middle of the grille meshing.

range. The muscle era was nearing its peak, and the GS was a big player in the game.

It was the cylinder head design that really generated the power for the GS400 engine. Compared with the so-called "Nail-Head" design used on earlier GS engines, these heads carried larger 2-inch-diameter intakes and 1.625-inch-diameter exhausts. The flow characteristics of the powerplant were also increased by the partial wedge design of the combustion chamber.

The '69 GS body style showed a slight revision from the previous year, with a curving body stripe reaching from the front quarter to the rear-wheel cutout and the "GS" as well as the "350" or "400" numeral markings were highly visible. The grille featured a single horizontal bar and vertical bars. Unfortunately, the performance and cosmetic changes were not enough to provide a large increase in buyers.

In 1970, things just couldn't have become any better. Performance was still the name of the game with the 350-ci engine edging up to a 315-horse rating, not far from the 1 horsepower-per-cubic-inch goal. The punchy mill acquired the rating at 4800 rpm, but was just as impressive from the torque point of view, with a 410-pounds-feet rating. As impressive as the 350-ci engine continued to be, it was lost in the hoopla of the intro-duction of a new 455-ci big block for the GS455. Yet,

the 455 didn't provide a big performance increase; its rating of 350 horsepower was just 10 horsepower more than that of the previous 400 engine. The big difference in the two powerplants came in the torque department, where the 455 excelled at 510 pounds-feet, possibly the highest ever in the muscle era, and made it at only 2800 rpm.

Buick officially called it the Gran Sport, but it wouldn't be long before the catchy GS name would be attached to the Buick muscle machine. The GS was first offered as an option, but later it would be a separate model.

The '70 GS's macho looks bespoke the performance that it carried under the hood. The twin scoops on the hood were functional and funneled cool air directly into the carburetor's air cleaner. Shown is a 1970 GS convertible.

As high as the 455's horsepower rating was, it was thought at the time to be lower than the engine's actual power output. For example, how could basically the same powerplant be quoted at 370 horses in the Riviera application? It came right down to the fact that insurance rates skyrocketed with horsepower increases on these Buick muscle versions. The increased displacement of the 455 was made by enlarging the bore from 4.040 to 4.315 inches, while the stroke remained unchanged at 3.90 inches. The 455 components were "full race," with wedge-shaped combustion chambers, aluminum pistons, forged rods, and a nodular iron crank. Topside, a 730-cfm Rochester four-barrel carburetor performed the fuel management functions, aided greatly by functional hood air scoops.

The weight of the GS455 was still a beefy 3,800 pounds, but with that 455 boiling under the hood, the performance was still awe-inspiring: 14-second/98-mph quarter-mile capabilities. Zero-to-60 could be accomplished in just over 6 seconds.

The 1970 model year also saw a new look for Buick performance models to accompany the new power. The GS455 was fitted with a GS455 emblem on the blacked-out grille. The model is considered by many to be one of Buick's top muscle models. Additionally, those hood scoops really gave it a muscle look.

For 1971, the 455 engine was back, but things just weren't the same. The cubic-inch displacement was still in place, but the horsepower took a dive to only 315. The compression ratio was reduced by 15 percent, which was the main reason for the power reduction. The 350 engine was also back for 1970, but it wasn't exactly the same. The engine's horsepower rating was lowered to 260 horsepower, a drop of 20 horses. Granted, the performance was down a bit, but make no mistake, these machines were still able performers on both street and strip.

The GS350 nomenclature was dropped for 1970, so the 350-powered cars carried only the GS name-tag, while the GS455 name remained intact. The GS455 emblems were also still in place, although Buick didn't officially use the nomenclature in its advertising.

Production totals for the '71 GS were almost identical to those of the previous year: 8,268 hardtops and 902 convertibles. Fortunately, even though the power was downgraded, the racy looks topside were retained. Included were bright rocker-panel moldings, blacked-out grille, still-functional hood scoops, and flashy trim. In 1972, the bottom dropped out for the GS, and performance was further reduced for the model, just as it was throughout the rest of the industry.

When you found a 1970 GS with the Stage 1 identification, you knew that you really had something. But if you are thinking about making the purchase of such a machine for restoration, make sure that you are getting the real thing because there are lots of phonies out there!

The Stage 1

The earlier GS models had performance; however, many buyers wanted more muscle unleashed when their right foot was stomped down. Fortunately, GM's former pure-luxury division was up to fulfilling that desire. Enter the so-called Stage 1 option. This pure-performance option kicked up the GS's already-potent performance so that it equaled or exceeded just about everything else on street or strip.

Even though the Stage 1 option was exactly that—an option—the name almost instantly stood on its own. You either had a Stage 1 car, or you didn't. As the years have passed, the attractiveness of these cars has only increased. The higher value of the Stage 1 has even caused a small number of GS owners to do a little

innovative conversion work on their standard GSs, turning them into bogus Stage 1 machines.

The Stage 1 modification was first offered on the 1968 GS400, as a dealer-installed option called the "Stage 1 Special Package," for race applications. The Stage 1 upgrades for this model year included a hotter cam, higher compression ratio, larger tailpipes, streamlined manifold, larger carburetor, and a Posi-Traction

rear end. The joke about the powerplant was that it was rated at only 5 horsepower over the stock 400 engine. Reportedly, it was also possible to acquire parts later included in the '69 Stage 1 package as dealer-installed components on the 1968 GSs.

For 1969, the Stage 1 was a factory option, obtainable by checking off the option on the order sheet. For the $199.05 price, a buyer received an unbelievable combination of performance goodies, a list of items that looked like it came from the local speed shop. The fact that a GS was a Stage car was noted under the hood with decals on the valve covers and air cleaner. The optional list of performance goodies included a custom high-lift camshaft, fast-flow fuel pump, a specially-calibrated Quadrajet carburetor on a cast-iron intake, and a high-pressure lubrication system. Exhaust was free flowing with a massive, 2.5-inch dual exhaust. The twin scoops on the hood were functional and pushed cool air directly into that big carburetor. A special linkage was designed to open the secondaries more quickly. The power was well applied to the pavement with a Posi-Traction rear end hooked with a 3.64:1 gearing.

The factory data indicated that the Stage 1 for 1969 had a rating of 350 horsepower at 5,000 rpm, a surprisingly minimal increase of only 10 horse-

There was no mistaking the distinctive induction system for the 1970 Stage 1 engine. The engine type was vividly announced by the Stage 1 name on the cleaner head itself.

This beautiful 1970 Stage 1 carries the optional

power over the stock GS400 engine. The torque for the Stage 1 engine was rated at an awesome 440 pounds-feet at 3,200 rpm. Performance Buicks were always noted for their punch at low speeds, and that was certainly the character of this machine. With the corporate battle for performance at the time, it's really surprising that more Stage 1s weren't built. With sales of only 1,256 cars, the 1969 Stage 1 was, and is, one of the most rare and desirable Buick musclecars.

But in 1970, a new most-desired model was introduced: the GS455 Stage 1. This powerplant was definitely the big kahuna. Among the upgrades included in the Stage 1 package were dual valve springs, bigger valves, a hotter cam, high-pressure oil-pump relief spring, and richer carburetor settings.

Its performance put this Stage 1 at the top of the big-gun musclecars of the era, actually being able to dip into the 13 second range at speeds in the 100-mph category, according to the car magazine tests. With

its 360-horsepower rating, this car wasn't an example of fuel economy, which averaged in the 12–13 miles per gallon range, depending how hard the driver put down his foot. These Stage 1s come rare, and they definitely are expensive in today's collector market.

rear-deck spoiler, which was extremely effective at high speeds.

Only 3,097 '70 Stage 1s were produced, and just 232 of them were the most desirable convertible models. The Stage 1 identification was now external, with "Stage 1" lettering right under the GS455 on the front fenders.

Nobody escaped the performance downgrades that started with the 1971 models, not even the Stage 1. Although the Stage 1 option would still be offered for several more years, like everything else during the power downturn, the Stage 1 went down with it.

A design highlight of the 1971 GSX was its body-length stripe that terminated by sweeping upward onto the spoiler. This graphic treatment gave the spoiler a look of being totally integrated with the body.

The GSX

Just when the 1970 GS455 Stage 1 seemed like the ultimate, along came the snazzy GSX model that same year. Quite frankly, it was an externally dolled-up Stage 1.

This first GSX looked like a combination of a rocket and a race car, with its snazzy body-length stripe that sported a kickup on the rear quarter. Broad stripes also swept down the scoop-infested hood with GSX decals in three external locations. In order to make this unique Buick really stand out, the 1970 version was offered in only two colors: Apollo White and Saturn Yellow. The majority of the initial GSXs were sprayed in the latter color. The GSX also featured an aft spoiler, a one-piece fiberglass unit that was bolted directly to the rear deck. In addition, there was also a fiberglass lower front spoiler, which was painted black.

Of course, that awesome 455 Stage 1 engine could be ordered with the GSX, but if that was too much power, a GSX with a more docile 455 engine was available.

The 1970 GSX had rolled out with little fanfare in national advertising. As a result, many potential buyers just didn't seem to know of its existence, so many of the 1970 GSXs were still sitting on showroom floors when the 1971s started to arrive. A total of 698 1970 GSX models were built. Well over half (479) were built with the Stage 1 option, with 280 of that number also getting the four-speed transmission. Reportedly, these particular GSXs were capable of 13-second quarter-mile performance.

Notice that the GS was still a part of the GSX model, but the GS was printed in smaller letters. There was no doubt that the company wanted the GSX to be a flashy performance model on its own.
It certainly succeeded.

The GSX was reduced to an option in its second and final year, 1971. Production was very minimal, a total of 124 vehicles. In order to acquire a GSX from the order sheet, the buyer had to check off the Special Car Order (SCO).

Nothing beats displacement, and Buick's 455 was top of the heap in 1970.

Check out the macho look of this 1966 Chevelle SS convertible. This black machine carries the matching blacked-out grille

Chevrolet—Classics with Real Power

Within the Chevrolet Division a large number of muscle models evolved during the musclecar era, and the same muscle powerplants were used in a number of them. Chevy's muscle models included Chevelle, El Camino, Nova, Corvette, Camaro, and Monte Carlo.

Chevelle

The trend toward ever-increasing horsepower started at Chevrolet in the early 1960s with the 409 power-plant. To remain in the game, the division realized it would have to punch up the performance of its mid-sized model line.

Chevy looked to Chevelle in 1964, with its macho Super Super (SS) model, as being a good place to start. Options such as a tachometer, sport steering wheel, chrome

That all changed in 1965. The magic numbers were suddenly 396 and 375, cubic inches and horsepower, respectively. Characteristics of the magnificent new engine included a forged crank, cast-iron heads, and an 800-cfm Holley carb, all decked out in a neatly detailed engine compartment.

The new heavy-hauler Chevelle was called the Z-16, and a number of significant modifications were made to be the Z-16 chassis. First, in order to accept the increased power and torque of the new engine, the frame was beefed up and a stronger suspension with new stabilizer bars was fitted. Other modifications included full-size 11-inch brakes, quicker steering, and special heavy-duty shocks and springs. Only 201 Z-16s were built.

The 396-powered Chevelle for 1966 (now called the "SS396") was a more streetable vehicle than the Z-16 had been. The standard 396 was now rated at 325 horses (50 horsepower less that the Z-16 396), but the optional L34 version was rated at 360 horsepower, courtesy of its special cam. Near the end of the year, the 375-horsepower L78 was offered. The 1966 SS396 featured simulated hood intakes, vinyl interiors, "Super Sport" script lettering on the rear quarter, and "SS396" emblems. A great year for Chevy, the SS396 model sold an impressive 72,272 units in both convertible and hardtop styles.

In 1967, the standard 325- and optional L78 375-horse ratings remained

with the centered SS letters.

trim items, and gauges gave the SS its sporting image. It was a great-looking machine, but there still wasn't that much power under the hood. Its 283-ci engine was good for only 195 horsepower. Even the mid-year introduction of a 327-ci engine didn't solve the horsepower image problem that the Chevelle was facing. The 327 was rated at a respectable 300 horses (a 250-horse version was also available), but the 327s were still a far cry from the big blocks that were now in the showrooms of the enemy camps.

unchanged. The optional L34's rating was reduced to 350 horsepower. Appearance-wise, the SS396 featured a blacked-out grille, "SS396" emblems, and other appearance options. Chevy built 63,006 SS396s for the year. The Chevelle SS was completely new for 1968. New appearance features included extensions on the lower body moldings, taillight panels, and a completely redesigned dash. The 325-horse powerplant was again the standard powerplant for the SS396 in 1968. The optional 340-horse L34 and 375-horse L78 versions were listed as options.

Slight appearance changes were made to the '69 SS. The big-block engine offerings were basically

The Z-16 was the first Chevelle to answer the musclecar call. Its 396 engine was rated at 375 horses. Only 201 Z-16s were built, and few have been located. Here's one of the best, the 1990 restoration owned by Harold Vieth of Iowa.

The look of the '67 Chevelle SS was little different from the previous year's model. Its front-end design was slightly changed, with a new horizontal bar grille. The 396 engine was a big selling point for the SS this model year.

The awesome 427-ci powerplant was first offered in the Chevelle for 1969. It was carried by both the COPO and Yenko (shown here) machines. With 425 horses, the powerplant would be under a Chevelle hood for only one year.

unchanged, but a new small-block option was introduced: the 300-horsepower L48 350-ci engine.

The most powerful of the Chevelles was not a completely factory-built machine. The so-called Yenko Chevelles were a special breed of the model that were modified by the Yenko Chevy dealership in Cannonsburg, Pennsylvania. Only 99 of the machines were built for 1969; about 35 of them are known to still exist.

The Yenkos were power personified with the awesome 425-horsepower L72 427-ci powerplant squeezed under

This '69 big block was the kingpin of the 396-ci engines. Three versions were available, with ratings of 325, 350, and 375 horses. The 375-horse engine is shown. From a twenty-first-century collector's point of view, this is the engine you want, and you'll pay a large sum of money to get it.

The flowing lines of the '70 Chevelle SS are clearly seen from this view. The body sides were completely devoid of chrome, with the exception of the SS letters on the front quarters.

the hood. There were also a number of additional appearance items added to the Yenko Chevelles, including special Yenko striping, Rally wheels, and extra gauges. In addition, there were a very few special Chevrolet Office Production Order (COPO) Chevelles built, all in 1969. These cars carried the same 427-ci engines as the Yenkos, and only a very few of these have been located; needless to say, these cars are very desirable to collectors.

Many Chevy performance fans consider the 1970 Chevelle the best and most desirable of the division's muscle machines. That opinion relates directly back to the introduction of the bone-jarring 450-horsepower LS-6 454-ci powerplant. The new engine came as a part of the SS454 option, and listed for a minimal $263.

The LS-6 used 11.25:1 compression heads, a special solid-lifter cam, aluminum intake, forged crank, and a giant 780-cfm Holley carb. A slightly lesser model of the 454 was the LS-5 version, capable of a reported 360 horsepower. Two potent 396 engines were available: the 350-horse L34 and the 375-horse L78. These 396 engines from 1970 and on actually had a displacement of 402 ci, but because of the aura of the 396 numbers, they remained in place.

Even as pressure mounted in 1971 to stop the production of big-block engines, the SS454s remained popular. Two 454 engines were once again available. For 1971, the LS-6 was rated at 425 horsepower and the LS-5 was rated at 365. Even though the sweet lines of the Chevelle body style were still in place for 1972, its performance was greatly decreased. The LS-6's rating was lowered by 25 horses. The LS-3 396-ci engine was also available, but it was a weak imitation of its earlier smokin' brothers.

The unique Cowl Induction hood was a significant attention-grabber on the 1969 El Camino SS. The classy truck was basically a Chevelle, except for the rear end.

El Camino

The El Camino truck conversion used Chevelle sheet metal and powerplants during the performance era. As such, it was possible to acquire a majority of the same high-performance engines of the Chevelle.

Model year 1970 was also the first year for the powerful 454-ci powerplant in the El Camino. Although the engine was publicized with the '70 Chevelle, it certainly deserves a second look in this car/truck application.

Nova

The sedate, domestic, and economical image that the Nova model carried during the early 1960s certainly made it an odd candidate for transformation into a performance model. However, during the last half of the 1960s, Chevy transformed this domestic model into a performance vehicle. By 1966, the Nova was available with the potent L30 275-horsepower version of the tried-and-true 327 powerplant. The real killer was the single-year L79 version of that same engine, which was capable of an impressive 350 horses. The L79's power, combined with the Nova's ton-and-one-half gross weight, made the model a real street performer.

The mainstay engine for the 1967 Nova was the L30 327-ci mill, which picked up 5 horsepower to total 280. The Nova SS body had been revised to give it the aura of a performance car.

For 1968, the L48 350-ci engine with a rated 295 horsepower was the standard powerplant. The SS350 package featured simulated scoops on the hood and a blacked-out grille and rear-deck panel, along with front- and rear-mounted SS tags. To increase that ever-important performance image for 1968, Chevy also equipped a limited number of Nova SSs with the awesome L78 375-horse 396. Even more exclusive was the optional L89 396, which was also rated at 375 horsepower, but was equipped with aluminum heads. The slightly less awesome 350-horse L34 396 was also available on the 1968 Nova SS. Just 667 Novas that year were equipped with the L78, 234 with the L34 and with the L89.

The L48 350 engine was rated at 300 horsepower for 1969, in a year where there were a minimal number of changes in the outward appearance of the SS. Quietly, though, it was still possible to acquire specially prepared Nova SSs that carried all three versions of the 396.

But as was true with the Chevelle and Camaro, Yenko modifications would also play here too, with the Yenko SYC 427 Nova. The engines were not factory-installed, but (like the Chevelle) squeezed into position by the aforementioned Yenko Chevrolet dealership. They were few in number, only 30 to be exact. The cars arrived at the dealership carrying the L78 396 engines, which were replaced by the L72 427-ci, 425-horsepower powerhouses. There were also reportedly a very few factory 427 Novas constructed. Only about a half dozen of these machines have been located, and their rarity makes them—along with the Yenko Novas—the most valuable of the Nova muscle models.

Probably the most desirable of all the performance Novas

For 1970, the standard engine for the Nova was a 300-horse version of the 350 engine, but the Nova could still be ordered with a big block. Although the L34 and L78 396 engines weren't advertised in the showroom literature, they could still be had on special order. There was yet another Nova for both 1969 and 1970, but it wasn't listed in any sales literature. It was called the Yenko Deuce and carried the LT-1 Corvette version of

was the Yenko "Deuce" version for the 1970 model year. Only 175 were produced that year.

the 350 engine, which knocked out 370 willing ponies. Other powertrain components included the Turbo 400 transmission controlled by a Hurst shifter and a 12-bolt 4.11:1 rear end. These models, of course, carried the distinctive Yenko body detailing.

Model year 1971 was the beginning of the end for high-power Novas, because the big blocks were discontinued and the remaining small blocks lost horsepower,

as Chevy lowered compression ratios in most of its engines. The new Rally Nova model featured a 245-horsepower version of the 350, while the SS version of the 350 was rated at only 260 horses on regular gas.

On the contrary, some data indicates that certain 1971 Novas were equipped with 454 engines. At that time, the 454s were available in Monte Carlos and Chevelles, but anything was possible.

Not only did the Vette have big horses under the hood, it also had great looks on the outside. The design featured a front end

Corvette

Many enthusiasts consider the Corvette a sports car versus a musclecar, a connotation that originated during the 1950s when the car was introduced with relatively small-displacement powerplants. That all changed in the 1960s when the model was fitted with some of the industry's largest and most powerful engines, making it one

carrying twin headlights, a vertical bar grille, and a sculpted hood.

The muscle era began in the 1950s for the Corvette, as proved by this twin-carbed 283-ci engine. This 1957 engine came in 245- and 270-horsepower versions. With a car weight of just over 2,700 pounds, this combination made for a real muscle machine.

of the top performers in the growing list of evolving musclecars.

The Corvette's 283-ci engine was capable of exactly 283 horsepower, some heavy performance for a machine weighing in at only 2,730 pounds. Dual-carb versions of the 283 powerplants were rated at 245 and 270 horsepower in 1958. A fuel-injected version made 290 horses. So it was made clear that even though displacement was low, the muscle era for the Vette really started in the 1950s.

By 1960, the fuel-injected 283 was rated at an impressive 315 horsepower. That high-performance option cost a healthy (for the time period) $484. The dual-carbed 283 horsepower rating peaked out at 275 horses in 1961.

Model year 1962 was significant for the Corvette because of the introduction of the 327-ci powerplant. The top fuel-injected version was rated at 360 horses. A pair of dual-carb versions were rated at 300 and 340 horsepower. The use of the familiar "L" engine designations began in 1963 with the L75 300-horsepower 327-ci, the L76 340-horsepower 327-ci, and the L84 360-horsepower 327-ci engines. Then, in 1964, the L84 power was increased by an additional 15 horsepower.

The end of the L84 came in the mid-1960s with the killer L78 396-ci powerplant. Although the 396

The 1962 Vette's front end had a macho look, with a blacked-out grille and other front openings. The headlight rims were done in body color, giving the model more of a street-machine look. Although many loved this body style, 1962 would be its final hurrah.

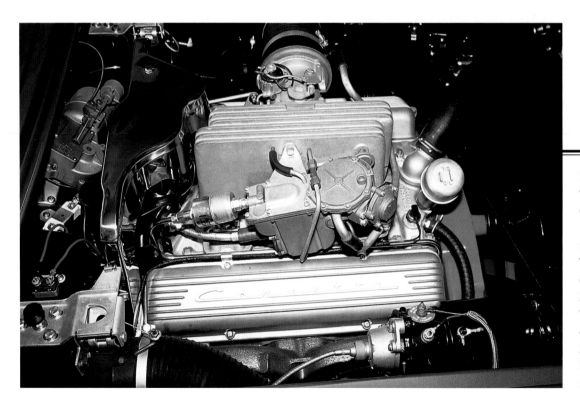

Fuel injection was a popular option for late 1950s Corvette powerplants. The two versions of the 1959 283-injected Vette mill were capable of 250- and 290-horsepower ratings.

One of the most popular Vettes ever built, the 1963 fastback Sting Ray design is considered a classic today. This particular example is powered by a 327-ci small-block powerplant. The front-end treatment was a dramatic change from that of the previous Corvette generations.

powerplants would prove popular in other Chevy models for several years, the L78 was only a one-year deal with Vette.

But this was the mid-1960s time period, and manufacturers couldn't sit still during the horsepower wars. The '66 Vette model year saw the introduction on two monstrous 427-ci powerplants. The L72 version was rated conservatively at 425 horses, while the tamer L36 model was advertised at 390 horses. A special "Power Bulge" hood came with the 427-equipped Vettes. The L72 powerplant had significantly more performance than the 396 L78, kicking the torque up from the L78's 415 to an unbelievable 460 pounds-feet. The L72 engine, which completely filled the Vette's engine compartment, featured solid lifters and was capable, according to *Car and Driver* magazine, of being a 12-second, 112-miles-per-hour performer on the drag strip. The standard L72 transmission was a four-speed.

But there was also significant small-block power for 1966: the 300-horsepower 327-ci powerplant.

Available with both three- and four-speed manual transmissions, a '66 Vette equipped with this engine proved to be a real sleeper performance model. Then came 1967, and the capable 427 had been kicked up a few notches with both 430- and 435-horse versions available, followed by the L68 400-horse model. With three carbs, solid lifters, and high-compression heads, the 435-horse L71 engine ($437 extra) was something else! In fact, many stated that the factory's horsepower rating was greatly understated. The L71 was the only Vette engine to ever use three carbs, and it was available from 1967 to 1969. If that wasn't enough, there was an aluminum head option for an additional $389. When equipped with that modification, the combination became known as the L89 and was rated at an identical 435 horses.

Finally, for 1967, there was the awesome L88 version, and there's an interesting story about this Vette model. It was a limited production model, and only 20 were produced its first year. Outwardly, the L88 didn't appear any different from any other 427 Vette, but fire

Two 427 engines were available for the 1967 Corvette, with horsepower ratings of 430 and 435, respectively. The model featured the lower body-length exhaust pipes. A convertible model is shown here.

it up, and you quickly learned this was a different beast. It wasn't built for the populace, but to race, and it was a tiger in Sports Car Club of America (SCCA) competition.

The engine featured an unheard-of 12.5:1 compression ratio, aluminum heads, four-bolt mains, aluminum pistons, forged rods, and a monstrous Holley 850-cfm carb sitting topside. Drag-strip performance for this machine was what you might expect, with elapsed times in the quarter mile close to the 11-second category at about 115 mph. Even though the L88 was never advertised for public consumption, there were still a limited

number that were purchased. One hundred and sixteen of the L88-equipped Corvette coupes were sold in 1969, its final year.

High-horsepower powerplants were back for 1968, along with a brand-new body design for the Vette. All the same 427 powerplants were available, but it would be the final year for the powerful engine. The top horsepower 327 in 1968 was the L79 version, capable of 350 horses, an option costing $105.

The big change for 1969 was the introduction of the new 350-horsepower 350-ci engine, designated the LT-1. Performance add-ons included aluminum

The 427 was called the L36 in 1967, and with the unique tri-carb setup, the engine was capable of 390 horsepower. The L71 427 included aluminum cylinder heads, and the horsepower increased to 435.

intake manifolds, high-compression heads, and an 800-cfm Holley four-barrel carb. For 1970, the power ratings of the LT-1 were kicked up 20 to 370 horses, some very heavy performance numbers for a small block. It wasn't cheap either, costing an additional $447 for the option. After 1970, the LT-1's horsepower rating started a steep decline. For 1971, it was back down to 350 and further reduced to a lowly 255 a year later. In 1973, it was completely eliminated.

In 1970, it would have appeared to the outsider that the horsepower race was continuing with the aforementioned 454 engine replacing the 427 family. Such was not the case, though, as only the 390-horsepower LS-5 version was available. The 454-powered Vettes had a sizable opponent, and it also wore the Chevy bowtie. The LT-1 was only 20 horses below the 454, and it was a much more streetable machine. For that and other reasons, just 4,473 LS-5 Vettes were built in 1970. However, the 454 hung around in reduced power versions until 1974. During this period, there was also a reported LS-7 454 powerplant, but the best sources indicated that the engine was never installed in any factory Vettes. Corvette experts surmise that some dealership installations could have occurred.

In 1971, a 425-horse version of the 454, the LS-6, was available. Even though the compression ratio had been appreciably reduced to 9:1, the powerplant was an excellent power-producer because of its large displacement, domed pistons, and 800-cfm Holley carb. The LS-6 proved to be a much better street engine than the early 427 powerplants. It would, however, be available for only this model year, and only 188 were built.

There are still those that will argue the Corvette was not a musclecar during this era. But judging by the powerful small- and big-block powerplants that were available, it's hard not to make the association.

The 1970 Vette differed little from the 1969 model. One of the biggest changes was the ice-cube-tray grille design.

The standard engine for this model was a 300-horse 350-ci engine.

The first Camaro made its appearance in the 1967 model year. With big horsepower and great looks, it was an instant winner. The SS got most of the attention, but there was also another version called the Rally Sport, or RS. The front-end looks of this first Camaro were stunning, as illustrated by this RS.

Camaro

Camaro buyers faced a difficult choice in the car's early years: Do I buy Trans Am race-derived Z28, the Super Sport (SS), or Rally Sport (RS)? Many buyers opted for the SS model, which provided the big horsepower capabilities. The SS was available with the Camaro in its initial 1967 model year. If performance was the name of the game, this was the option to pick. For the really big horsepower numbers, however, buyers had to wait a bit during the model year.

When the SS package was first introduced, it came only with the L48 350-ci engine, producing 295

horsepower. But that would all change mid-year with the introduction of a pair of 396-ci big blocks: the L35 punching 325 horses and the L78 with 50 more than that. The L35 was fitted to 4,003 Camaros that year and the L78 to 1,138. Maybe the latter wasn't surprising, since the buyer had to plunk down an extra $500 for the additional horsepower.

The L48 350 mill provided plenty of power for the 12,476 buyers that bought the 295-horse version. Although it was not available with the SS option, mention should be made of the L30 327 powerplant, which was available in both 1967 and 1968 and produced 275 horses. The SS Camaros also came with a dynamite

This '68 Camaro has just about the best of everything. First, it's the top-of-the-line SS model, as identified by the SS on the front quarter. Then, there are those magic 396 engine-displacement numbers, an engine that was available at several different power levels.

This Hugger Orange and White '69 SS Camaro really lit the racing fires, looking like it was ready to take to the track. The design was highlighted by the wide pair of body-length stripes and the twin louver set on the aft hood.

In an amazing occurrence, two of the first three Camaros were given the huge honor of being the pace car for the Indy 500. This is the 1969 version, and the lettering on the door leaves no doubt of its selection. A number of replicas were built (this being one of them) and were powered by a 350 engine.

suspension system. Big-block SS Camaros also came with heavy-duty engine mounts, rear axle, and clutch.

The SS emblems seemed to be everywhere on the body, sitting in the middle of the blacked-out grille, gas filler cap, and front quarters. When the 396 was ordered, the front-quarter SS badge was replaced with a special 396 Turbo Jet emblem located directly under a Camaro nametag. Throw in the custom hood, blacked-out rear panel, and SS striping, and this was one killer machine. The popularity of the muscular SS continued in 1968, and although the body style remained basically unchanged, there were some subtle changes made. First, instead of the SS emblem embedded in the vertical bumblebee stripes, the number "350" or "396" engine displacement numbers were used.

There was also the so-called "Big Engine" hood, which featured a pair of twin metal inserts featuring four simulated carburetion stacks.

Also for 1968, Chevy offered a third 396 powerplant for the Camaro SS: the L35. The L35 was rated at 350 horsepower, halfway between the 325- and 375-horse models. In addition, for the ultimate performance enthusiast, there was the L89, the special 396 mill equipped with aluminum heads, larger valves, and a custom Holley carb. Introduced late in the model year, only 272 were built. Four four-speeds and a pair of automatic transmissions were offered for use with these engines.

Nineteen sixty-nine was the final year of Camaro's first generation, and this year saw the production of the

Several different small-block 350 engines were fitted to the 1969 Camaros, and this 300-horsepower version is one of them. It carried the company name of Turbo-Fire. This particular engine powered a 1969 RS.

It wasn't a well-known fact, but a small number of 427-powered Camaros were built. Some of these were factory-built versions called COPOs; others were built by performance dealerships such as Yenko (shown here), Berger, and others. Yenko was the most prolific, with its distinctive body trim and detailing. These models are certainly valuable and exciting.

GM pony car billow to 243,085. Camaro's third year looked a lot like its earlier cousins, but there were some refinements with a lightly altered sheet metal sporting sharper bends and curves.

It was again a year of performance with the three optional 396 engines offered for the SS. The standard powerplant was the L48 300-horsepower 350-ci engine, which became a popular choice. The super-rare and super-powerful L89 engine was still available in 1969, but only 311 customers checked off the option. That's not surprising since that engine option cost an additional $710.95, which was about one-fourth the cost of the basic Camaro model.

The 1969 SS option was identified by RPO Z27 and cost an additional $295.95. It included front disc brakes, heavy-duty suspension, the custom hood backed by insulation, wide-oval tires, black and bright accents, detailed engine compartment, and the expected SS badges. A limited number of SS COPO models were built this model year with either factory- or dealer-installed 427 powerplants.

Big changes were instituted in the 1970 model year, but it took awhile to get production started before the new body style was introduced, therefore causing it to be called the 1970 1/2 Camaro. For many, the wait was worth it, while others yearned for the first-generation styling.

The design changes for this first of the new era were significant. The full body-wide grille was gone, replaced with the centered rectangular design, and the headlights were now located outside its confines. The same powerplants of 1969 were again available for 1970. The L48 350 engine was also a popular option because it offered good performance combined with street manners (a Road & Track road test showed a capability of 86 miles per hour and 16.6 seconds in the quarter).

A number of the Chevy intermediate and big models in 1970 got the big-block 454. Chevrolet even considered putting that engine in the Camaro, but it didn't happen, although there were a small number of dealer installations. The L48 300-horsepower 350 was a part of the SS option, which also included special accents, power brakes, hood sound insulation, blacked-out grille, and SS emblems on the rear deck, grille, and front quarters.

The '71 Camaro was pretty much an external duplication of the previous year. The downturn in performance was evident as 30 horses (10 percent of the previous year's 300-horse value) were clipped off the L65 powerplant's horsepower rating. A 396 (its actual displacement was 402-ci) could be ordered as the LS-3, but only 1,533 Camaro buyers selected that powerplant option. The SS, costing an extra $313.90 in 1971, included the expected features, but the SS identifying emblems were only on the front quarters and steering wheel.

Monte Carlo

Luxury and elegance were two of the big goals of Chevy engineers when they introduced the brand-new Monte Carlo in 1970. Those goals were certainly achieved, but the Monte Carlo also ended up with one other significant characteristic in certain models. When some big engines were dropped under these particular Monte Carlo bonnets, the model became a musclecar of sorts, but its performance was far from that of its Chevy brothers because of its extra weight.

The Monte Carlo was introduced quite late in the musclecar era, and therefore, it didn't have that muscle image for long. The model was immediately provided with the 454 engine, so there was no long buildup in power. It got the biggest there was in the Chevy camp right off the bat. That 454 power, the LS5 360-horsepower version being the standard offering in this application, was definitely needed since the Monte Carlo weighed in the neighborhood of 3,500 pounds. It certainly was no match for the other performance cars of the day. Car-magazine tests of the day showed it only had a 16-second capability in the quarter mile. However, if you wanted to plunk down the extra bucks, it was possible to order the 390- and 425-horse versions of the 454.

Besides special suspension equipment, the SS454 package also included the Turbo Hydramatic transmission and power disc brakes. A black and silver lower trim stripe carried the SS454 designation. Fewer SS454s were sold in 1971, making Chevy wonder if it had made a big mistake with the introduction of the model The LS-5 was the standard engine for the '71 SS454, with a horsepower rating of 365 horsepower, although the 425-horse LS6 could be ordered as an option. Non-SS Monte Carlos were available with the 245-horsepower 350 and 300-horsepower 402 engines. For the 1971 model, it was as though Chevy was trying to hide the fact that big horses were resting under the longest hood in the Chevy inventory. There was no SS454 identification anywhere on the front of the top-line model to announce its big-block pedigree. Even the emblems that were on the car were practically invisible.

In 1972, the performance-oriented Monte Carlo was stone dead. In fact, anything to do with

The Monte Carlo appeared late in the musclecar era and had several faces. With its stylish stance and impressive front end, it gave the impression of being a luxury car, but with the addition of the powerful 454 engine, there was also a muscle connotation to this machine.

performance or a racy image was actually mocked in the Monte Carlo national advertising campaign. A greatly degraded 454 powerplant could still be ordered, but it was only putting out 270 net horses. The last year for the 454 was 1975, but by then its horsepower rating had dropped off by half.

When the 396 was no longer big enough, Chevy introduced the even larger 454. There were two versions of the engine, the LS-5 (shown here) and the awesome LS-6, with 360 and 425 horsepower, respectively.

Oldsmobile 442s and Ws

Like the other GM divisions, Oldsmobile certainly didn't want to get shut out of the musclecar game, and came forth with its first muscle model: the 442. Several versions of the 442 soon followed, and each soon earned its own fame.

The 442

Everywhere, three-digit numbers flaunted the cubic inches of the giant powerplants they carried (including SS396, 421HO, 440 Six-Pack, and so on). The numbers "442" in Olds lingo meant something entirely different than engine displacement, or even torque. It came down to a specific meaning for each number. The first "4" stood for the four-barrel carb, the second "4" identified the four-speed fully synchronized transmission with floor-mounted shifter. Finally, there's that last elusive "2." It quite simply stood for the stock dual-exhaust arrangement.

The initial 1964 442 had only 330 cubic inches under the hood, but before the 442 performance era ended, the cubic inches would numerically top the 442 name by 13 cubic inches.

National advertisements proclaimed the 310 horses and 355 pounds-feet from the so-called Jetfire Rocket V-8. This engine featured an impressive 20-horse increase over previous engines of the same displacement, and that extra power really showed itself in performance. Reportedly, the 0–60 time was in the mid-7-second range. Oldsmobile ads touted the excellent handling of its new 442, and the bragging was justified. Heavy-duty springs up front were rated at 410 pounds per inch, while the impressive rating out back was 160 pounds per inch.

Surprisingly, the first 442, like the first Pontiac GTO, was not a separate model. Rather, the 442 was an option for the F-85 Cutlass line. It was called the B-09 option, or Police Pursuit Apprehender, and cost an additional $289.14. With the superb publicity the initial 442 acquired, it was not surprising that Olds engineers would kick up the ponies a bit more for the following 1965 model year. All the 1964 goodies were once again included, but the 330-ci powerplant was replaced with a 345-horsepower 400-ci/screamer. Both the bore and stroke were appreciably increased for the new powerplant, to a 4-inch bore and a 3.98-inch stroke.

Was the 1970 Hurst/Olds an out-of-sight, macho looker of an Olds musclecar? You better believe that

it was, decked out in basic white with gold trim on the fenderlines and on the center of the hood. Check out those brutish twin hood scoops, which scream big-time performance.

Model year 1964 was the first year for the 442, but it was an option package for the Cutlass, not really a separate model. The numerals "4-4-2" denoted a four-barrel carb, four-on-the-floor transmission, and dual exhausts. In the years to follow, not all 442s would carry all those attributes, but the popular designation would still be used.

Compression ratio remained extremely high, at 10.25:1. The new engine was topped with a 700-cfm Quadrajet carburetor, along with a special radiator, 70-amp battery, and dual low-restriction exhausts.

In 1966, the optional L69 powerplant with three two-barrel (300-cfm each) carbs was similar to the famous GTO Tri-Power. A number of these powerplants were retrofitted by dealers and owners. The standard 442 powerplant was again the 400-ci engine, only this year the rating was increased to 350 horsepower, nudged upward by its new 10.5:1 compression ratio.

Only slight changes were made to the body styling with blacked-out tail panel and grille. The 442 emblems were quite noticeable, located on the right rear deck, rear quarters, and grille.

The 442 for 1967 was starting to gain its own distinctive look with a unique grille accented with an embedded 442 emblem. The characteristic fender scoops were gone for this year, but the model now also sported new sport striping on the doors and fenders. The aggressive look was set off with new redline tires. The tri-carb setup of the previous year was gone for 1967, but the 350-horse, four-barrel 400 engine with 440 pounds-feet of torque was still available. Also, powertrain upgrades allowed the awesome engine to operate at a much higher efficiency level. A special Turbo Hydra-Matic transmission, a stronger 12-bolt rear end (available with 3.42 and 3.91:1 ratios) and F70x14-inch wide-oval tires made the '67 442 a street performer of the first order.

Buyers loved the automatic transmission, and it outsold the four-speed model for the first time. The 442s were also starting to turn heads on the national drag strips, and one even set a National Hot Rod Association (NHRA) B/Pure Stock national record.

Several car magazines voted the 1968 442 as the top performance car of the year, and it was well deserved. The package included a 325-horsepower engine under the hood, heavy-duty suspension, front and rear stabilizers, and wide-oval redline tires.

For 1968, the news was big in the 442 camp—and for two big reasons. First, the 442 became a separate model on its own, no longer an F-85 option. It even had its own new body style with a 3-inch-shorter wheelbase at 112 inches. The December 1967 *Motor Trend* magazine report described the model as a "Stirring car, full of built-ins and potential for performance enthusiasts." The 400 engine was back again in redesigned form, with a larger bore (4.125 inches) and a considerably smaller stroke (3.385 inches).

This red air cleaner denoted the standard power-plant for the '68 442, a super street and strip performer kicking out 325 horsepower from its 400 ci. With a 10.5:1 compression ratio, four-barrel carb, and dual exhausts, this powerplant was one of the top muscle performers of its time.

Horsepower was quoted at 350 horses with a four-speed transmission and 325 with the automatic.

For the 1969 model year, the 442's body lines remained relatively unchanged, but there was a considerably different look to the front end. The grille was halved by body-colored sheet metal upon which was scribed the expected 442 identification. The 442 numerals were also boldly blocked out on the front quarters.

The 442 body design was slightly altered for 1970 and appeared to project more of a refined look. The changes were greatly appreciated by the buying public. The rear bumper carried four slotted vertical taillights, located directly over the stylish dual exhaust extensions. Olds also offered the optional rear-deck-mounted W-35 spoiler.

Additional refinements were made to the front end, including a new vertical pattern in the twin grille. Next came a pair of macho hood scoops on the new W-25 hood, and the neat thing about the scoops was that they were functional. A pair of racing-style hood pins added to the performance look. It's easy to understand why many 442 enthusiasts will tell you it didn't get much better than the 1970 442!

The top engine displacement for 1970 was the W34 455 engine with a 4.125-inch bore and a 4.250-inch stroke. Its horsepower was rated an impressive 365, produced at 5,000 rpm. Also, its unbelievable rating of 500 pounds-feet of torque spoke for itself.

Yet there were even more options available to handle the horsepower of this heavy hauler. The M40 Turbo Hydra-Matic with the W-26 Hurst dual-gate shifter was a potent combination for the strip or street. The FE3 sport suspension was also state-of-the-art.

Olds ads of the time period understandably put this model on a pedestal. They stated, "Beneath that air scooped, fiberglass hood rumbles as large a V-8 as ever has been bolted into a special performance, production automobile . . . The special hood? It's part of the W-25 package you can order. Do so—while you're still young enough to enjoy it!"

But things started changing with the 1971 model year as the American lust for performance seemed to be fading. Maybe the country just lost the mood for hot cars in the environment of the upheaval of the Vietnam War. Apparently, Olds started to go along with that trend of non-performance thinking as the tire-scorching capabilities of the 442 started its downward spiral in 1971. However, Olds wasn't alone when it started

yielding to the trend. It was happening everywhere. In previous years, 442 production had accounted for as much as 5 to 6 percent of the total Olds production. In 1971, the 7,589 442s produced accounted for only a miniscule 1.3 percent of the Olds total. Despite these changes, the '71 442 didn't look that much different from its year-earlier muscular brother. That rakish twin-scoop hood, complete with the hood pins, was still in place, and there was a new mesh grille design, which was the only significant external change.

On the whole, major changes were taking place across the industry in the powerplant department. The culprit was low-octane unleaded fuel— something that high-compression engines certainly didn't care for one bit! Also, government-mandated pollution controls were putting a clamp on performance. In order to utilize the wimpy gas, it was necessary for Olds—along with all the other GM divisions—to drop the compression ratio figure by two full digits. That's a bunch, and it's amazing that the horsepower didn't drop more than it did. The power loss in the 455 powerplant was minimal: 25 horses to a still-impressive 340 figure. It was the final year that horsepower was quoted in gross numbers.

For 1972, "performance" seemed a dirty word. The new trend evolving in Olds advertisements was obvious when engine performance wasn't even mentioned until you were almost done reading the ad. "442" this model year meant "A special 442 Sport Handling Package" that could be ordered on four different Cutlass models. The term "package" in those ads indicated bad news for the 442 as a separate model. After four years as a distinct model during the true muscle era, the 442 was reduced to option status again.

It was not expensive to have your '72 Cutlass garbed as a 442: $71.62 for the Cutlass and $150.61 for the

The '69 442 was styled for the track. The front end featured a pair of blacked-out openings and a slotted front bumper. The sheet metal was sculpted on the sides, with a macho kickup on the rear quarters. Rakish five-spoke wheels were a final touch to this performance fantasy.

Cutlass Supreme. Both included the Hurst three-speed shifter. The package also included body and rear-deck striping, louvers, and the expected trio of famous number identification. Suspension pieces (carried under the FE Rallye Suspension Package) were heavy-duty springs and shocks, front and rear stabilizer bars, heavy-duty rear lower control arms, and 14x7-inch tires.

New government regulations, high insurance rates for big-engined cars, and the turn toward lower-cost cars had automotive designers looking in different directions. The '72 442 was really starting to feel the pressure. The standard '72 442 powerplant (the L-75) was rated at 270 horsepower. Remember again, those were net horses, so the reduction in performance wasn't as bad as the reduction in numbers would suggest. The equivalent gross-horsepower number was probably approaching 300 horses.

Even in this era of performance downgrading, the 455 engine was still offered. In fact, that engine would be available through the 1976 model year.

For 1969, the GS was offered with a pair of punchy mills: A 400-ci engine producing 340 horsepower at 5,000 rpm and the 350-ci engine shown here, which was capable of 280 horses. Even though the 350 had fewer cubes, it was still capable of impressive performance.

Externally, the fact that a particular '69 442 carried the W-30 option was not loudly announced. The W-30 designation was in the body-length striping directly under the 442 numbers on the lower front quarters. Its extra performance certainly deserved more significant attention.

Olds "W" Cars

The best way to describe the "W" was "Wild"! That was certainly the case with the number of W versions that spelled performance in a big way for certain 442s and other Olds models.

In the early twenty-first century, such W-modified machines are the most coveted and most valuable of the Olds performance line. Initially, there was no W on the external sheet metal, but Olds quickly realized that 21st letter identification should be announced for all to see, and the W appeared on later versions. With the initial Olds W machines, it was necessary to lift the hood to firmly ascertain the performance breed. In all, there were three Olds W variants. The most popular was the W-30, along with the W-31 and W-32 versions.

W-30

The W-30 was the most abundant and most recognizable of these Olds performance options. It was offered from the mid-1960s through the early 1970s, only on Olds models, and the package's equipment really set the W models apart from standard Olds performance machines.

The 1966 442 was the first recipient of the W hardware. Interestingly enough, the initial W-30 was added to an existing powerplant that really didn't need it. The powerful L69 442 engine was already hooked with a tri-carb setup and sure didn't look like it needed any additional ponies. That didn't stop some Olds performance types who added the package to the already potent mill.

The W-30 addition consisted of a unique dual-snorkel air cleaner with a trio of twin-nut depressions.

The muscle era was going away, but the W-30 was still offered for the 1972 model year. The performance decreased with a drop in compression ratio that year, but the W equipment made it about as good as it could get.

The 5-inch-diameter air cleaner openings hooked to a pair of hoses that traversed forward, outward, and then dropped to lower-bumper openings. Dark, elongated scoops were quite evident in the bumper and subtly indicated what was under the hood. The name of the system was appropriately known as the "Force Air" induction system. But there was more W-30 stuff for 1966. When the W-30 option was ordered with the 400-ci engine, the 440 was fitted with stouter valve springs and a hotter cam, which optimized the powerplant for the W-30 induction system.

Olds benefited in national drag racing when a W-30 L69 won the National NHRA C Stock titles—pretty heavy stuff for the first time out! It's hard to believe that Olds didn't flaunt the W-30 on the car's exterior, but it just didn't happen. So, only the really

tuned performance nuts knew about it. That, however, would change in the years to come.

One would have thought that the increasing exposure to the W-30s would have caused the Olds big wigs to vigorously announce its presence, but that wasn't the case in 1967. For 1967, the W-30's second year, the L69 tri-carb engine was gone, so the air cleaner was now mounted on a Rochester four-barrel and it carried a more conventional round air cleaner with a removable top.

Also, a dealer-installed option presented some full-race modifications. The Force Air Induction system was still in place, but there were some changes in the system. A significant modification was required to route the left side tubing. The battery had to be removed to make room, and it was relocated to the trunk. To further enhance the performance of W-30 cars, Olds engineers

The W-30 option was available with the 455 engine for 1970. The W componentry on this awesome powerplant provided an extra 5 horsepower over the standard 455 mill, possibly much more. The engine was also significant because it had a torque capability of the magic 500 pounds-feet figure.

trimmed a little weight off in a very innovative way: the fiberglass inner fenders were bright red in color. Other subtle changes in the W-30's second year made this machine a real performer on the strip, capable of sub-14-second quarters. A new capacitive discharge ignition system supplied a hotter spark, and a hotter cam with a longer 308-degree duration provided a fatter charge of fuel and air. The restyled and rakish A-Body design went right along with the power image of the W-30 option for 1968. Also, for the first time, you could even read about the W-30 in the company literature and discover what that magic designation actually meant.

Interestingly enough, there was a note to potential buyers about the rough idle characteristics of the W-30 powerplant and that it might not be ideal for all buyers. Despite that, 1,911 performance-oriented buyers selected the W-30 option. You can bet that every one of those buyers wishes they still had that car today!

For 1968, the induction ducts were moved from the grille to underneath the bumper, and the air cleaner configuration was changed to a twin-snorkel version of the standard 442 air cleaner. Despite the changes, the W-30's power rating was unchanged: a sizzling 360 horsepower. In all, the W-30 componentry added 35 horsepower to the standard 442 powerplant.

The W-30 option included more than just a fancy induction system. Tolerances were extremely tight on W-30 engines, and these engines were mated to limited-slip rear ends that carried ratios up to 4.66:1.

For 1969, the W-30 option was available only on the 442. The 400 powerplant was souped to the hilt with dual air ducts, dual-intake air cleaner, big intake and exhaust valves, and a high-overlap cam. Even with all the upgrades, the horsepower was still listed by the factory at 360. This was the first year that Dr. Olds, a devious-looking character, was used in W-30 advertising.

For 1970, the W-30 got the 455 engine. The W-30 components were awarded 5 extra horsepower (370 at 5,200 rpm), a very conservative addition. The trademark induction tubes were replaced by the twin-scoop W-25 fiberglass induction hood. The brand-new 455 featured hydraulic lifters, five main bearings, and dual exhausts

The final year for the W-31 was 1970. Hood scoops replaced the characteristic induction tubes of previous years. Horsepower was advertised at 325, the same as for the standard 442 powerplant, even though the W-31 mill sported an aluminum intake manifold.

that helped it earn a monumental torque rating of 500 pounds-feet at only 3600 rpm. The impressive performance numbers compensated somewhat for the '70 W-30's weight of almost 3,700 pounds.

The '70 W-30 was the ultimate of the W mods in the minds of many collectors. Unfortunately, it was but a final fleeting moment because a serious downturn in performance commenced the following year, as a two-point drop in compression ratio lowered the horsepower rating of the mighty W-30 powerplant by 70 horses to 300.

W-31

For 1968, Olds first offered the W-31 option with the Cutlass and F-85, which souped up small-block powerplants with the same parts and pieces that made the W-30 as great as it was. Interestingly enough, the W-31 option was not available on the 442, which of course carried the Olds performance image. With a twin-snorkel air cleaner, 2-inch-intake heads, and a four-barrel Rochester carb, the W-30's engine produced an impressive 320 horsepower.

The first W-31 engine was called the Ram Rod 350, which was identified with a fender-mounted decal depicting the end view of two pistons, rods, and a crank with the words "Ram Rod 350."

For 1969, the changes were minimal and production was up slightly to 931 units. It was also possible to acquire a W-31 convertible, but few buyers made that choice. A W-31 decal on the front quarters was the only identification. The engine carried a four-barrel Quadrajet carburetor. Its horsepower was increased by 5, to 325.

The W-31's final year was 1970, but that certainly hadn't been the plan of Olds brass. Nevertheless, the 1970 W-31 was the best of the three years the model was in production. New features included chrome medallions and a redesigned fiberglass hood sporting Ram-Air scoops that fed cool air directly into the top of the air cleaner.

W-32

The W story still had one more twist and turn. The W-32 model, which lasted for only two years (1969 and 1970), is often forgotten when the W cars are mentioned.

Looking down the side of this 1968 Hurst/Olds, a number of the unique features are visible. Note the black striping that runs two-thirds the length of the body, terminating at the front bumper. Also, under-bumper

The model was a mid-1969 introduction and was strictly a 442 option, and even then was available only with the 400 engine and Turbo Hydra-Matic 400 automatic transmission.

For the 1969 W-32, the only identification was the W-32 decals located directly above the front quarter marker lights. The W-32 400-ci engine was rated at 350 horses and was fitted with a 286-degree duration, 0.472-inch lift, 58-degree overlap cam, and the Force Air system with the under-bumper scoops. Other unique aspects of this gutsy powerplant included separated center exhaust ports and individually branched exhaust manifolds. The only external identification was a W-32 decal affixed directly above each front-quarter marker light.

In 1970, the W-32 was not available with the 442; instead, it was offered only on the Cutlass Supreme.

During that year, the W-32 option included a 455-ci engine mated to an M-40 automatic. For some reason the W-32 decals were deleted, making it somewhat of a lost W machine. Nevertheless, its performance certainly wasn't lost on the select few who ordered the option.

Hurst/Olds

Any mention of the magical name "Hurst," and all kinds of visions come into focus—performance, style, class, and Linda Vaughn! Fortunately for the Olds line, the red and blue block "H" with the oval-encircled "Hurst" featured on a series of specially prepared Hurst/Olds models boasted big-time performance and out-of-sight appearance innovations. The name also carried a solid connection with fans of the musclecar. The

We're talking about a killer powerplant with the '68 Hurst/Olds mill, a 455-ci performer that was capable of punching out an impressive 390 horses and 500 pounds-feet of torque. The powerplant was fitted with hydraulic lifters, 10.25:1 compression ratio, and a high-performance crank and camshaft.

scoops were used to duct cool air into the twin-snorkel air cleaner.

Hurst/Olds models appeared six times, but only two times during the muscle years, in 1968 and 1969.

The initial 1968 Hurst model (H/O for short) was just the ticket for the Olds image, and through the years the model has become one of the most desirable of all the vintage muscle models. The biggest of many attractions on the Hurst model was what rested under its bawdy black and silver hood: 455 cubic inches of W-30-style big block pumped out 390 gross horsepower at only 5000 rpm and 500 pounds-feet of torque at 3600 rpm. The engine carried the W-30 Force Air Induction system, with snorkel tubing and under-grille scoops, a high-lift cam, and special carburetor jetting.

With a rear sway bar and heavy-duty suspension components, the 1968 Hurst/Olds also had superb handling. New front disc brakes, equipped with a proportioning valve, added greatly to stopping efficiency. Slap on the Goodyear G70x14s and stand back! The performance was breathtaking. With the 3.91:1 rear end ratio, quarter-mile capabilities were in the high-13-second bracket.

If buyers liked the '68 Hurst/Olds for its radical performance looks, then the '69 Hurst most likely completely blew them away. Where the first H/O's sinister gray and black paint was somewhat drab, the '69 Hurst was a ray of sunshine in gold and bright white. With the white as the base coat, a wide gold band swept across the lower body, along with pointed gold stripes on the upper front and rear fenders, twin stripes up the rear deck, and a single stripe on the hood. This vehicle was a knockout!

The awe-inspiring W-30 455 mill was still in place, but for some reason, Olds now announced its performance at a 10-horse-lower value of 380 horses. The torque was still listed at the same 500 pounds-feet. The March 1969 edition of *Car and Driver* magazine documented 14.1-second, 100-mph performance in the quarter mile.

A LeMans option in 1964, the GTO would soon be a model on its own, and what a model it would be!

Pontiac and the GTO

Among the GM brands, Pontiac probably shares the top performance image with Chevy. That image was forged by the Grand Prix models and burnished by the GTO, The Judge, and the Firebird/Trans Am models that evolved in the late 1960s and early 1970s.

The GTO

The 1964–1966 GTOs constituted the first generation. They have become muscle classics of the first order and will always hold their high place when the first musclecars are recalled. It could be said that the GTO came to being on a technicality. In the early 1960s, the Pontiac division operated under an edict that restricted it to fitting standard engines of 330 cubic inches or under. At some point, somebody figured out that the

The top-gun powerplant for the '64 GTO was this Tri-Power 389, which had a vacuum setup for bringing the two outer carbs on line. Unfortunately, the system didn't work that well. For that reason, many owners replaced the factory setup with a mechanical linkage. When perking to perfection, the Tri-Power engine was capable of 348 horses. A four-barrel version of the powerplant produced 325 horses.

the famous Tri-Power. The Tri-Power's three Rochester 2GC carbs provided a total of 780 cfm and an additional 23 horsepower at 4900 rpm.

Pontiac also upgraded the suspension system of the GTO to include a four-link upper and lower rear control arm setup, augmented with heavy-duty coil springs. The front end was fitted with a beefy 15/16-inch stabilizer bar. It should be noted that this first GTO was actually not a model on its own, but an option of the LeMans model. Even so, its long, flowing body lines combined with a twin-opening blacked-out grille to set the standard for the classic muscle looks of the early GTOs.

Years later, the 1965 GTO was voted the most popular GTO of any of the 11 versions produced from 1964 to 1974. The four-barrel 396 engine was now rated at 335 horses, the increased performance coming from a higher-lift 288-degree cam. Minor changes were also made in the head and intake-port deck heights, and a Carter AFB four-barrel carb was now standard. The same

restriction applied only to standard engines, and not to optional engines. One of the first products of this loophole was the GTO, a combination of the new-for-1964 A-body chassis and tuned 389 big-block engines.

Two quick-revving 389-ci powerplants were available in the GTO. They would remain in place, basically unchanged for the GTO's first three years. One version carried a standard four-barrel carburetor, while the big-publicity version carried a row of three two-barrel carbs,

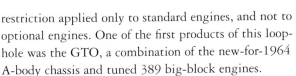

The 1966 GTO sported a revised front end that gave the third-year GTO a completely new look. The grille recesses were deeper, and the parking lights were mounted on the grille-opening mesh material. The grille recesses were also outlined with chrome trim. That infamous GTO name was buried in the left grille recess.

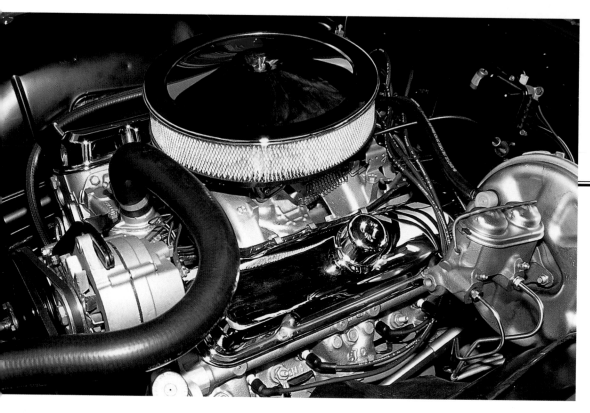

Sadly, the triple carbs were gone after 1966, but the 400 HO power-plant shown here was a worthy replacement. With a special cam and valve-train, the power-plant was rated at 360 horses.

The 1965 GTO was definitely built to attract the youth culture. It was quite different from the 1964 and 1966 versions.

three Rochester two-barrels were again in place for the Tri-Power version, but the 1965 version was rated at 360 horsepower, 12 more than in 1964. The major appearance change in the model was the stacking of the headlights.

For 1966, louvered taillights were the major appearance change. The popular twin-opening grille remained unchanged.

Bigger changes were made for 1967. The body was restyled, and a 400 replaced the 396 in the engine compartment. Compared to the old 396, the new 400 engine featured a larger bore and redesigned cylinder heads. In standard form for the GTO, it was rated at 335 horsepower. Yet, for some reason the 400 just didn't seem to have the charisma of the 389, which had generated a cult following.

The new 400 engine was also available as the 400 HO, which was rated at 360 horses. Drawing on some older classic Pontiac technology, the headers were quite similar to the earlier Super Duty versions of the early 1960s. A hotter cam and open-element air cleaner also added punch to an engine that would soon have performance enthusiasts exclaiming about its virtues.

But if you really wanted to light your fire,

you had to try the other 400 engine, the 400 Ram-Air. Even though the 400 Ram-Air wasn't fitted with the three two-barrels of the Tri-Power 396, it was given a functional hood scoop, a hotter cam, and 4.33:1 rear end. Despite all these additions, the 400 Ram-Air was rated at the same 360 horsepower as the HO.

For 1968, the GTO featured a completely restyled chassis with bumpers made of Endura plastic. In its application to the new front-end design, the flexible space-age material was able to absorb low-speed front-end impacts and bounce back to its original shape. In a bold update, the headlights were hidden in blackout grille openings with lids opening when the lights were activated. The centered single hood scoop of the previous year was replaced by dual scoops.

Horsepower was plentiful from three monster powerplants. The standard 400-ci engine was uprated to 350 horses at 5,000 rpm with an awesome 444 pounds-feet of torque. The HO and Ram-Air 400s returned with a few refinements in 1968, but the same power ratings as it had in 1967. A series of automatic and manual transmissions, along with numerous rear-end ratios, could be assembled for just about every customer's performance fantasy.

For 1969, the name of the GTO was fitted with an Endura bumper that would assume its original shape after an impact. In 1970, the taillights were installed in the rear bumper. A decal on the rear deck identified the GTO.

Late in the '68 model year, Pontiac kicked up the power again, replacing the Ram-Air 400 engine with the new Ram-Air II powerplant, which sported a hotter cam, new round-port heads, a Rochester Quadrajet carburetor, a hydraulic cam, and forged aluminum pistons. It was rated at 366 horsepower. Although the Ram-Air induction system was a factory option, it was not installed at the factory. Rather, it arrived in the trunk for dealer installation. All these changes for 1968 won the GTO Car and Driver's award for the Best All-Around Car and Best Sports Design.

Next, for the final GTO of the decade, Pontiac made appreciable changes to the GTO's exterior, the majority of them to the rear end. The vertical portion of the rear

deck, including the taillights, was completely encased with chrome stripping.

For the 1969 model year, the so-called Ram-Air III engine replaced the Ram-Air II. Updates to the III included D-Port heads, all-weather ram-air scoops that could be closed off in case of rain, and a Rochester Quadrajet carburetor. Making 366 horsepower and identified with Ram-Air decals, the Ram-Air III was another rocket, slightly faster than the Ram-Air II of the previous model year, and capable of a magazine-tested best quarter-mile clocking of 14.10 seconds.

Ask any GTO performance enthusiast and you'll quickly learn that the Ram-Air IV, introduced in 1969, was the ultimate of the 400 engines. With many

upgrades—including aluminum heads, a hotter cam, stiffer pushrods, all-weather Ram-Air system, and four-bolt mains, the Ram-Air IV was beautifully balanced and a terror for any confrontation. The fact that it was rated at only 4 horsepower over the Ram-Air III was a joke!

Many said that the '69 Ram-Air IV was the fastest of all the muscle GTO versions. Capable of 6.6-second performance to 60 mph, the IV could cut the quarter mile in less than 14 seconds.

For 1970, the big GTO news was the initial use of a 455-ci powerplant. The big block would be around through the 1973 model, but with greatly reduced power. In 1970, however, the 455 HO was rated at a very respectable 360 horsepower. It could be ordered with either a three- or four-speed manual or the Turbo Hydra-Matic transmissions. Also available were the standard, Ram-Air III, and Ram-Air IV 400 engines. Strangely, it was also possible to order the Ram-Air equipment with the 455 engine, but there were no internal engine changes made when that engine choice was made. Surprisingly, the new 455 wasn't making the horsepower expected from its greater displacement. Rated at "only" 360 horsepower, the 455 was less powerful than the Ram-Air 400-ci powerplants. Appearance-wise, the 1970 GTO's more aggressive and deeply recessed grille and dramatic sculptured side sheet metal transformed the car's look. Although horsepower ratings were down throughout the industry for 1971, the GTO for that year was still muscle-bound, even after meeting strenuous new emission requirements for the year and modifications for the car to run on lower-octane regular gasoline.

General Motors decided that the best way to cope with the new low-power petrol was to lower compression ratios. Needless to say, it required a significant lowering. For the 455 engines, compression was reduced to a lowly 8.4:1. Emissions were further reduced for 1971 on the 455 HO engine by sealing the carburetor's mixture-adjustment screw and adding a new sensor arrangement that shut the automatic choke off more quickly during start-up. With all these changes in the name of economy and reduced emissions, performance fans dreaded to hear what effect the changes would have on quarter mile clockings. For sure, the good old days with high 13-second runs would definitely be a thing of the past. What the changes actually meant in terms of horsepower was a drop to 300 (from 350) for the 400 engine and to 335 for the 455 HO.

Styling-wise, the '71 GTO took on a completely new look in the front end. It was actually more racy looking than the '70 model, even though the 1971 engines couldn't back up their looks like the 1970 engines could.

In the years to follow, GTO performance grew steadily less impressive. Yet, during its day, the GTO was right up there with the best, in both performance and appearance.

An interesting footnote must be added to the GTO story, one that didn't take place in the factory: During the 1960s, a number of dealerships specialized in performance upgrades of existing GM models. Royal Pontiac, of Royal Oak, Michigan, was the prime Pontiac dealership for such activities, and its products became known as "Royal Bobcats." Small name medallions on the front quarters identified the GTOs that were so endowed.

Royal Pontiac offered a number of performance packages during the 1960s GTO performance years. Most notable of these was the substitution of a 421-ci engine for the stock 389 engine. These replacement engines were created at over 400 horsepower. Other modifications included the tweaking of the stock engines for greater performance. In 1968, Royal offered a 428 HO engine swap for only $650. A March 1964 *Car and Driver* test of a GTO Bobcat with the 421 engine showed amazing performance of 13.1 seconds at 115 mph in the quarter mile.

Compared to the total GTO production, the numbers of the Royal Bobcats was small, making them a great investment in the twenty-first century. Basically, an already great muscle machine was made to be even better.

Color styling for the first 1969 Judge was considerably different from the final two versions. A distinctive multi-colored stripe stretched from the front of the fender and followed the line of the windows, terminating on the high rear quarter. It really spruced up the conservative GTO exterior.

The Judge

Returning to the pure factory GTOs, there has to be mention made of the Judge, which was basically a gussied-up GTO. Even so, it was a GTO model that stood on its own. You owned the Judge, not a GTO!

Pontiac transformed the standard GTO into the Judge halfway into the 1969 model year, with the intention of making it a single-year model. Its popularity prompted Pontiac to keep it in the lineup through the 1971 model year. The reasoning behind the Judge design was that the new GTO variation might attract the younger set with its visual appeal, specifically garish colors and unique detailing. "The Judge" emblems on each front fender, on the right side of the 60-inch-wide rear spoiler, and on the dash set this special car apart

Eye-catching "The Judge" emblems on the front fenders and on the rear deck spoiler announced that this was not a regular GTO. When the model was discussed, it was called "The Judge," and not the "GTO Judge."

The biggest difference between 1969 and 1970 Judges is in the side-stripe design. Where 1969 models had a single stripe stretching two-thirds the length of the body, 1970 Judges had two eyebrow stripes. A 60-inch-wide spoiler across the rear deck really set off this machine.

from the more pedestrian GTOs. A distinctive stripe that swept along the top of the front fenders, across the doors, and finished in a flared kickup further distinguished the Judge.

In addition to visuals, performance was an equally important part of the formula for the Judge, so the initial 1969 model carried the Ram-Air III powerplant. The even-more-potent Ram-Air IV was also an option. Officially released to the public in December 1968, the comparison to the standard GTO was quickly made by the buying public. The lineage was definitely there, but it looked like a distant cousin, and it was a rowdy cousin at that!

The first 2,000 of the '69 Judges were painted an eye-catching Carousel Red, but later the Judge was available in any GTO color. The Judge cost just over $300 more than the equivalent GTO.

An even-more-distinctive look came on board with

This 1970 Judge was fitted with the same 366-horsepower 400-ci 366-horsepower Ram-Air III engine that was available on the '69 GTO.

1970's Judge. A pair of twin eyebrow stripes, located on the front and rear fenders, anointed each side of the car. "The Judge" decals appeared on the lower front fenders and on the right side of the rear deck.

For the final 1971 model, the Judge remained basically unchanged from the previous version. The same teardrop striping was still in place, and the fact that the vehicle was carrying the LS5 455 HO was announced on each edge of the rear spoiler. An interesting footnote on 1971's Judge must be included: 15 models were produced in Cameo White with black striping and rear wings. The cars were built under RPO 604, and their extreme rarity makes them highly desirable to collectors.

The Firebird and Trans Am

The Firebird was the first Pontiac trip into the sports-car market, but it was created under a significant design handicap. The division was forced to design its first Firebird, and a number of succeeding models, with Camaro sheet metal. But even with this constraint, the early Birds had a distinctive look of their own.

The first Firebird, introduced in 1967, featured horizontally mounted headlights resting within the recesses of a distinctive blacked-out grille. The rear of the Bird was also unique, never to be mistaken for the Camaro. In that first Firebird, the top-performance small block was a 285-horsepower 326-ci powerplant. It was a part of the HO option, which cost an additional $280 and which included appearance and performance items.

Several experts have stated that the HO engine might have approached the 300-horse figure. Looking at the engine components—Carter four-barrel carb, dual exhausts, and a 10.5:1 compression ratio—might tend to verify that opinion. The HO body was also distinctively signified with a body-length horizontal stripe and an embedded "HO" identification.

But if you wanted the top-dog performance engine of the 1967 Birds, the Firebird 400 was the ticket, with an offered choice of two different 325-horse engine versions. The Ram-Air version, which added an additional $263 to the option sheet, featured functional hood scoops. Hood scoops were also included with the base 400, but they were non-functional. Both engines were rated at 410 pounds-feet of torque.

Nineteen sixty-eight would have to be called a year of subtle refinement for the Firebird; if you didn't look carefully, it was really difficult to detect the external

Changes were minimal for the 1968 Firebird, but when you've got a winner design, why mess

differences between the two model years. The major difference was body side marker lights (in the form of the Pontiac medallion) that appeared on the rear quarters. The 350 HO powerplant provided a pleasurable punch with an impressive 320 horsepower. The numbers were great for a small block, and close to the high-performance standard for the day of 1 horsepower for each cubic inch.

A pair of 400-ci engines proved to be the hot tickets for the 1968 Firebird line. The standard engine was

with success? This side view shows a '68 Firebird convertible and the sculpting running down the side of the machine.

called the Firebird 400, but to really light your fire, there was the Ram-Air version. Again, there was minimal difference horsepower-wise, only 5 to be exact, with the Ram-Air version rated at 335 horses at 5,000 rpm. A second version of the Ram-Air engine was introduced near the end of the model year, the Ram-Air II. The Ram-Air II might have been called an upgrade, but it was effectively a new powerplant. It was definitely full-race, with four-bolt main bearings, special manifolds, and forged pistons.

Nineteen sixty-nine was also a year of transition. Most importantly, 1969 was the model year that the Firebird line established itself as a distinct model, no longer just a sheet metal copycat of the Camaro. This distinction was accomplished through a complete restyling, both inside and out. Next came the introduction of the Ram-Air III and Ram-Air IV powerplants.

Also important was the introduction of the high-level Trans Am model, which would prove to be the star of the Firebird line in the years to come. The Trans Am was

The first Trans Am was introduced in 1969 and sometimes carried both the Firebird and Trans Am names on the front quarters. The L-67 was the standard engine for the Trans Am, but the car could

available in only one color combination, a smashing white base color complemented with a pair of body-centered wide blue racing stripes. The base Firebird 400 carried the potent 330-horse W-66 engine (an output that was only 5 horses more than that of the 350 HO engine).

The 400 engine was capable of considerably more torque at 430 pounds-feet versus 380 for the 350 HO.

The next step up was the 335-horse Ram-Air 400 engine, which could be ordered under option code 348. Carrying the L-74 engine designation, the Ram-Air 400

be ordered with the more-powerful Ram-Air powerplants.

carried a special de-clutching fan. A point of confusion existed with this engine, as it basically was the famous Ram-Air III, along with also being called the 400 HO. Whatever it was called, it required buyers to cough up $435 for its purchase. Also, as in the GTO, the Ram-Air IV L-67 engine was available. Ram-Air IVs were rated at 345 horsepower, but the engine's torque rating was the same as for the Ram-Air III.

In 1970, the new Formula 400 made its appearance, and it was available with both the base 400 (330

During the early 1970s, the Firebird line presented a number of models that flaunted both styling and performance. The integration of air dams into the lower front end is evident in this photograph.

The '69 Ram-Air III L-74 engine (shown here) was available with the first Trans Am and was advertised with a 335-horsepower rating. The Ram-Air IV offered an additional 10 ponies and is considered the ultimate by collectors.

Although performance was down for the 1972 Firebird, the looks were still there. With those twin blacked-out grilles and those hood-hugging scoops, it just didn't get any better!

For the 1971 Firebird, engine displacement was up to 455, and the 455HO LS-5 made good use of the displacement, with 355 horsepower at 5,200 rpm. The engine featured an 8.4:1 compression ratio and a functional cool-air induction system.

Whether a '73 Firebird was carrying the SD-455 powerplant or not, this was a great-looking machine. Note the

horsepower) and the Ram-Air III (now advertised at 335 horsepower). It was also available with the Ram-Air IV, although that engine had to be special ordered.

Trans Ams for 1970 featured a single stripe on the center body, but the color scheme was flipped and featured a blue body with a white stripe.

In 1971, there was a continuation of Firebird performance, even though it was supposed to be the downturn year because of the new smog retirements. On the contrary, 1971 was the year big-block 455 engines were introduced. The two trends just didn't seem to mesh. It was interesting to note that the 455 displacement figure for the Firebird exceeded the maximum 454 number for the Camaro line.

The Trans Am for 1971 looked very much like the previous year's model, but the standard powerplant was the 455 HO engine, with an identifying decal on the shaker hood scoop.

The LS5 455 was the top powerplant for the model year, with the net horsepower figures rated at 300. When the net figure quoted for 1971 is converted to the gross figure previously quoted, however, the figure approaches 330. Quarter-mile performance was still in the 14-second bracket.

In an amazing change of direction, the 1973 and 1974 model years saw Pontiac introduce its out-of-step LS-2 SD-455 Super Duty engine. Internally, this was a full-race mill, which the division had advertised as

molded lower front spoiler and the flairs directly in front of the rear wheelwell opening.

having 290 net horsepower and 395 pounds-feet of torque. Right in the middle of the gas crunch, this powerplant seemed completely out of touch with the atmosphere of the time period.

Nineteen seventy-three saw the introduction of the powerful 455 Super Duty engine, at a time when the muscle was dropping off in just about every other model. The horsepower was advertised at 290, a figure that was grossly underrated. The NHRA listed the powerplant at 375 horses, a more reasonable figure in the minds of most.

Chapter Two

Ford Muscle

Every once in a while, Detroit produces a vehicle that hits the right button at the right time. Through a combination of superior styling, improved engineering, market conditions, good luck, or maybe the position of the planets, sometimes a vehicle rolls out of the plant and into America's heart.

Such an event took place on April 15, 1964, when the Ford Motor Company released its new Mustang, a personal car that offered sporty looks, performance, and attitude. And all of it was offered at an incredibly affordable price. What was Ford thinking? That maybe it could recoup some of the money spent on developing the Falcon. Using as many parts as possible from that popular economy car would help spread the immense costs incurred during development and production of a new car. If another vehicle could amortize tooling costs, profits would roll in that much sooner.

The original pony car changed the American automotive land-scape forever. Although the Pontiac GTO is recognized

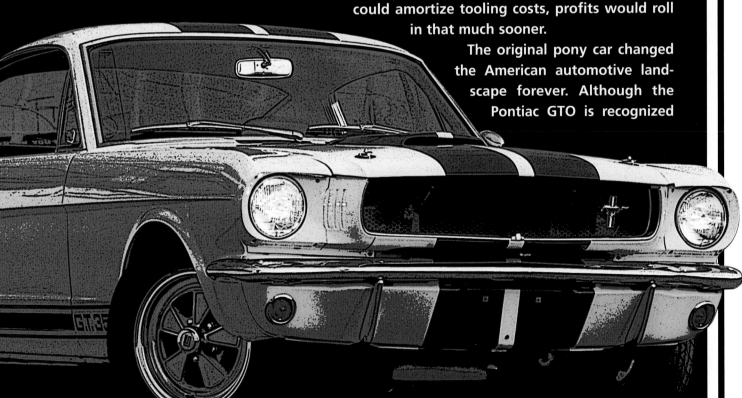

Built on April 20, 1964, this Mustang Pace Car replica is one of only 190 made to commemorate the 48th annual Indianapolis 500-mile race. The release of the car was accompanied by a well-planned media blitz. By the end of production year 1965, Ford had sold more than 600,000 hardtop, fastback, and convertible Mustangs. Note how the factory stripe ended at the end of the hood and did not run under the bumper.

as the first musclecar, Ford sold 500,000 Mustangs in its first year. After that first year's raging success, the high-performance youth market could no longer be ignored. Chrysler and General Motors jumped on the bandwagon and developed their own pony cars. Eventually, the competition created the glorious musclecar era. Since 1964, Ford has had a Mustang on top or near the top of the high-performance heap. The long list of legendary high-performance cars includes the Shelby GT350, the Boss 302, the Mustang SVO, and the Cobra R, just to name a few. This book is a celebration of Ford's greatest high-performance Mustangs.

The Ponycar that Sparked a Revolution

From humble beginnings, the mighty Mustang was born. As engineer Bob Negstad recounted, it was created "from floor sweeping." Ford planning manager Hal Sperlich teamed with Ford division boss Lee Iacocca to

use the Falcon as a starting point. As Iacocca put it, it was a car that "you could drive to the country club on Friday night, to the drag strip on Saturday, and to church on Sunday."

With the unibody Falcon as the platform, Eugene Boridinat, Ford's styling director, organized an internal Ford styling competition. The winning entry, penned by David Ash and Joe Oros, was called the Mustang. It continued the Ford trend of naming vehicles after animals, such as the Thunderbird and Falcon. Base price was only $2,320.96, a price virtually anyone visiting a showroom could justify. Mustang "Job One" rolled off the assembly line only 571 days after the prototype got the green light. At the time, no one could have imagined the success it would achieve or its far-reaching impact on the automotive landscape.

The 1964¹/₂ Indy Pace Car Coupe

It was a perfect day in May in Indiana, the kind that the local chamber of commerce waxes poetic about in vacation literature. A race was being held in the state capital, the kind of race that the world waxes poetic about. And pacing the "Greatest Spectacle in Racing" was an automobile that the motoring press was waxing poetic about, an automobile that captured the enthusiasm of the times—the Ford Mustang.

Production was going full steam, yet the backlog of orders grew. Master marketer Lee Iacocca wanted to increase the new car's profile even more. When Ford made the decision to use the Mustang as the pace car for the 1964 running of the 48th annual Indianapolis 500-mile race, Ford found itself in an enviable position, but it couldn't afford to specially produce the 38 convertible Mustangs needed for pace car duties. Every vehicle made was being rushed to buyers. So Ford went to its local Indianapolis dealerships and "procured" the needed cars.

All 38 pace cars were fitted with 289-ci V-8 engines, the largest V-8 in the lineup. Three Mustangs were set up for actual pacing duties, featuring the "Hi-Po" 271-horsepower 289-ci K-code engine and Borg-Warner four-speed. An increased capacity oil pan and radiator were part of the package. The cars were fitted with a heavy-duty suspension and Koni shocks to cope with the high speeds. The other 35 pace cars were in essence festival cars. A stock D-code 289-ci V-8, producing

210 horsepower, resided under the cars' hoods. A four-barrel carburetor and either a four-speed manual or an automatic transmission was also part of the package. The interior was red, white, or blue vinyl. All 38 Pace Car Mustangs were painted Wimbledon White, paint code M, and had pace car graphics and blue racing stripes.

To honor the Mustang's role and to increase public awareness, approximately 190 Mustang pace car replica coupes were built in April and early May 1964. Ford ran a "Checkered Flag" sales contest among its dealerships; the winners were awarded a pace car replica. Unlike the actual pace cars, the coupes were painted Pace Car White, paint code C, and all of them had the same mechanicals. An F-code 260-ci V-8 engine carried a two-barrel C40F-9510-B carburetor. It produced 164 horsepower at 4,400 rpm, and torque came in at 258 foot-pounds at 2,200 rpm. Each replica was fitted with the three-speed Cruise-O-Matic automatic transmission, power steering, back-up lights, AM radio, and a white vinyl interior with blue accents. The sides were adorned with the same graphics enjoyed by the actual pace cars, and like all early Mustangs, the replicas differed from 1965 Mustangs in a number of areas. When the pace car replicas were rolling down the assembly line, a worker

All 190 pace cars were fitted with the 260-ci V-8 rated at 164 horsepower. It was a sprightly performer and was the start of a long line of impressive small blocks. Note the generator that was installed on 1964½ vehicles; alternators were installed in the 1965 model year.

would write the words *PACE CAR* on top of the radiator support to identify the vehicle to other line workers.

Ford never officially built a 1964-1/2 model. Any Mustang built between March 1964 and August 17, 1964, is known as an early Mustang. About 150 items are unique to early Mustangs, such as the use of a generator, driver's footwell carpeting without a vinyl toe pad, and a nonadjustable passenger seat. Other features special to early Mustangs included smaller 4½-inch fender emblems, seat belts anchored to the floor with eyebolts, and lower-pitched, larger horns. The Pace Car coupes were exactly like their production line brethren in regards to equipment fitment.

As the introductory year progressed, Ford ramped up production to satisfy the public's demand. The exposure gained at an Indy 500 on Memorial Day, 1964 only fueled the phenomenon that was to be the Mustang. Little did anyone know that the Mustang would become something of a regular at the famous 2.5-mile oval.

The 1965 GT Convertible

From the early days of the automobile industry, manufacturers have known that the buying public would ask for more power, better handling, and the styling to set them apart. Mustang buyers wasted no time asking for more, and Ford was ready with more tempting treats. One of the first started with a *K*.

Ford had slipped its Hi-Po 289-ci engine into the Indy Pace Cars that actually saw high-speed duty on the

With the introduction of the GT option in 1965, performance took a big leap forward. A tiny emblem on

Ford used red-white-and-blue vertical bars with the horse emblem, so onlookers would know that this is an American horse, not a foreign one. The lavish use of brightwork in the interior was a common 1960s styling touch. The simulated holes on the spokes of the steering wheel were meant to evoke a sports car feel.

the front fender told spectators that the potent K-code 289-ci engine was under the long hood. The high-revving engine produced 271 horsepower at 6,000 rpms.

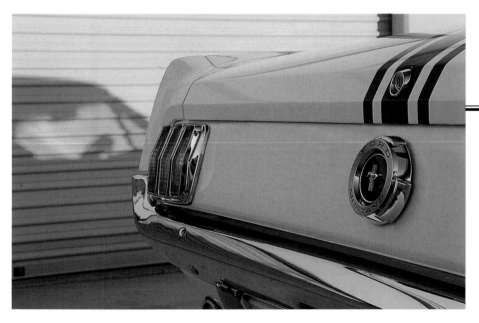

The first-year Mustang established the short trunk lid and long-hood pony car tradition. The center filler for the fuel tank stayed in the center of the rear panel for many years. Three vertical taillights continue to be a Mustang trademark. The stripe ended at the rear of the vehicle at the same position as on the nose.

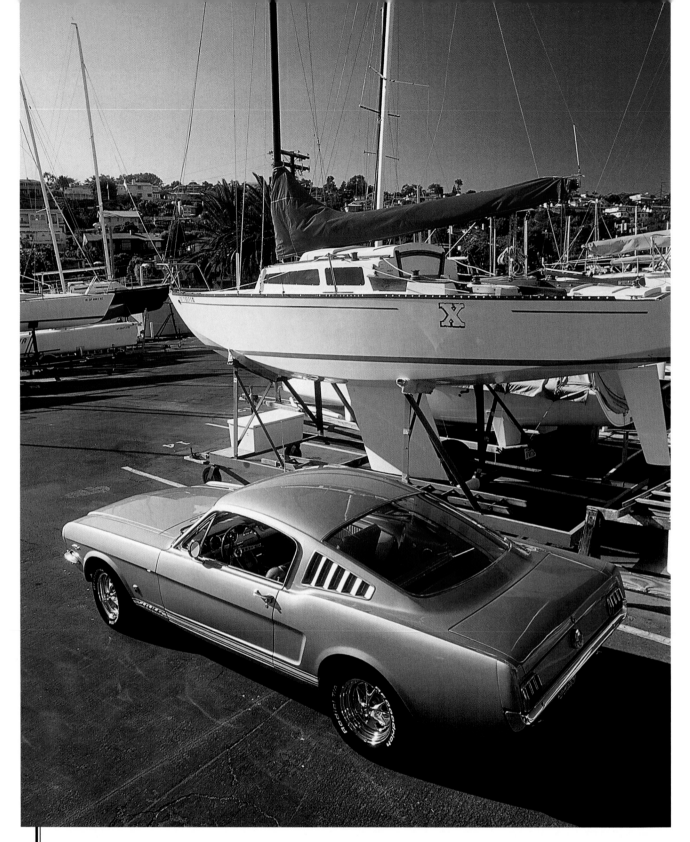

The fastback model provided a great blend of a graceful form and function. The classic lines and tasteful styling made automotive history and influenced car design in the years that followed. The folding rear seat gave an impressive amount of storage room, and the large rear window flooded the interior with light.

These extractor vents on the C-pillars were functional, helping to pull air out of the passenger space. For 1965 the rectangular speedometer was replaced by the round dial speedo, which better supported the performance car aura. The rim of this steering wheel is made of real wood.

With almost 1 horsepower per cubic inch, the 289 small-block V-8 quickly became a legendary engine. The quick-revving powerplant featured a 600 Autolite four-barrel carb, cast-aluminum pistons, and cast-iron block. With 271 horsepower on tap, it would match the performance of a Chevrolet 327.

track. The Hi-Po K code engine was the first high-performance step in the Mustang's long history. It became available to the public on April 17, 1965, and was just one component of Iacocca's "Total Performance." As part of the GT Equipment group, the 271-horsepower engine could fill the engine bay for $276.34. The small-block screamer could make the 6.95x14 Dual Red Band nylon tires lay down impressive black stripes. With its 10.5:1 compression ratio, premium fuel was mandatory. It developed 271 horsepower at 6,000 rpm and 312 foot-pounds at 3,400 rpm. Topped with a 600-cubic feet per minute (cfm) Autolite four-barrel carburetor, the black painted iron block had a bore and stroke of 4.00 by 2.87 inches with slightly domed cast-aluminum pistons. Mechanical valve lifters with dual valve springs helped achieve the high engine speeds. The nodular cast-iron crankshaft, along with the 1-13/16-inch thick harmonic crankshaft balancer kept the engine in one piece. Threaded rocker arm studs, modified connecting rod bearings, caps and bolts, and a

low restriction air filter helped produce power on cue. Handling ignition was a mechanical-advance, dual-point distributor.

More power meant more demands on the suspension. The front long-arm/short-arm suspension was fitted with heavy-duty springs, raising the ride rate from 82 to 105 pounds per inch. The rear leaf springs were massaged as well, the ride rate increasing from 101 to 130 pounds per inch. The front stabilizer bar was beefed up from 0.69 to 0.84 inch. The result was a significantly firmer ride, and the 16:1 ratio steering (stock ratio was 19:1) made changing direction a more hurried evolution. The Hi-Po also had a heavy-duty rear end differential with a 9-inch rear axle ring, rather than the 8-inch unit installed in all other Mustangs.

The result of all this engineering work at Ford became clear on the road. In the October 1964 issue of *Car and Driver*, a 271-horsepower 289-ci V-8 Fastback Mustang was put through its paces. With a 4.11:1 rear axle ratio, the 'Stang hustled down the quarter-

Ford wanted a bona fide production race car to compete in SCCA (Sports Car Club of America) road racing. So Ford partnered with Carroll Shelby, and together they built one of the greatest sports cars of the 1960s— the 1965 Shelby GT350. The glamour the GT350 brought to the Mustang line was immeasurable, and the

race car image as well as performance helped sell a lot of street cars.

mile in 14.0 seconds at 100 miles per hour and bolted from 0 to 60 in 5.2 seconds. Top speed was recorded at 112 miles per hour, and the front Kelsey-Hayes 10.0-inch ventilated disc brakes "passed our fade tests and simulated panic stops easily," the magazine said. In the pages of the September 1964 *Road & Track*, a 271-horsepower Mustang with a set of 3.89:1 gears clicked off 15.9 seconds at 85 miles per hour in the quarter-mile.

Behind the wheel, the GT driver saw a different view than that of standard Mustang owners. A five-instrument cluster featured a 140-mile-per-hour speedometer in place of the regular Mustang 120-mile-per-hour unit. When the Interior Decor Group option was ordered for $107.08, two more gauges were installed—an 8,000-rpm tachometer and a clock. A full-length console was installed as well. More options allowed the buyer to equip the Mustang GT as close to country-club cruiser or racetrack terror as the buyer wanted.

By the end of the 1965 model year, 680,989 Mustangs had been built. Out of that lofty figure, only 7,232 were equipped with the K-code 289. While relatively rare, the $276.34 K-code option was a hell of a first step on the performance ladder.

The 1965 Shelby GT350

Ford wanted to race the Mustang in Sports Car Club of America's (SCCA) production race car class, but Ford's efforts weren't successful. Lee Iacocca discussed the dilemma with former race car driver and team owner Carroll Shelby. Shelby said he could build the minimum number required and get busy winning in the B-Production class if Ford would make 100 Mustangs available to him quickly. Before he could say *race*, Shelby was working in a shop near Los Angeles International Airport putting together the package that would become the GT350.

Ford built the "knocked down" (incomplete) vehicles in two days in San Jose, California, and shipped them to the Shelby hangars where the cars were completely outfitted. All of the cars were fastbacks with white exteriors and black interiors. Ironically, these hangars were some of the facilities used in the production of the North American P-51 Mustang fighter plane from World War II.

When the cars arrived, they were modified rather substantially, especially in the suspension department. The upper A-arms of the front suspension were lowered

To make the GT350 the best handling car possible, Shelby extensively modified the stock Mustang suspension. It featured lowered upper A-arms, large 1-inch roll bar, traction bars, and high-performance shocks. The small hood scoop was functional. The bumpers were largely decorative; most racers pulled them off before starting a race. The hood pin locks were necessary in holding the fiberglass hood down during the triple-digit speed excursions.

1.0 inch, and the standard 0.625-inch antisway was replaced with a beefier 1.0-inch unit. The rear suspension was fitted with override traction bars, and Koni shock absorbers were installed on each corner. Standard Mustang front disc brakes were teamed with Fairlane station wagon 10-inch rear drums with sintered metallic competition pads.

The engine did not require extensive modifications. The small-block 289-ci V-8 proved to be strong and durable. Shelby wanted more than strong. He got it. An aluminum high-rise intake manifold and a 715-cfm Holley carburetor, part number S1MK-9510-A, were installed. This carb was fitted with a center pivot float that would not stick against the side of the float bowl under heavy cornering. The stock heads were removed, ported, and polished. Every reciprocating part was balanced. A custom-ground camshaft was installed, with 306-degree duration, .457-inch lift, and 78-degree overlap. A finned aluminum oil pan, holding 6.5 quarts, increased lubricating capacity. Exhaust gases were shown the door through Tri-Y tubular headers, routed through glass pack mufflers before exiting in front of the rear tires. After all the modifications were made, the 289 pumped out an incredible 306 horsepower at 6,000 rpm and 329 foot-pounds of torque at 4,200 rpm.

Built to compete at venues such as this, the 1965 GT350 was a justifiable legend in its own time. Notice how the racing stripes extend down to the bottom of the valence panel, unlike the Pace Car replicas built at the Ford factory.

The Shelby team took the already powerful 271-horsepower 289 and turned it into a voracious monster cranking out 306 horsepower at a lofty 6,000 rpm. The King Kong 289 featured ported and polished heads, custom-ground camshaft, Tri-Y headers, and a plethora of other high-performance parts. The car achieved 0 to 60 times under six seconds. Note that the circular rod connecting the inner fender wells was a device meant to stiffen the front suspension and improve handling.

The Shelby GT350 featured a well-appointed and purposeful interior with the requisite wood steering wheel and burly shifter. In order to save weight, rear seats were not installed. Wide competition seatbelts gave a hint to the purpose behind the wheel. The large tachometer mounted atop the dash helped the driver monitor engine speed without taking the eyes too far off the road.

The gearbox was a cut-and-dried choice—an aluminum-case, Borg-Warner T-10 close-ratio four-speed. At the other end of the driveshaft lurked a Detroit Locker limited slip differential with 3.89:1 gears standard, but 4.11, 4.30, or 4.57 gears could be substituted. A set of 7.75x15-inch Goodyear Blue Dot tires, good for 130 miles per hour, provided traction. The stock steel hood was replaced with a fiberglass unit, complete with a functional hood scoop. The back seat was also removed and was replaced by a one-piece fiberglass shelf with a storage point for the spare tire.

About 200 pounds were shaved off the stock Mustang weight. Atop the dashboard went a Delco tachometer and an oil pressure gauge. The battery was installed in the trunk to balance the weight distribution for the first 325 vehicles, then it was moved to the engine compartment due to occasional fumes in the interior. Wide seatbelts and a wooden steering wheel were some of the finishing touches. All of this sold for only $4,547!

The performance numbers tell the story. *Motor Trend* tested a GT350 in its May 1965 issue and it ripped down the quarter-mile in 15.7 seconds at 91 miles per hour. The sports car rocketed from 0 to 60 miles per hour in 7.0 seconds, while stopping from the same speed took 140 feet.

And were the results worth the work? Trophies, trophies, as far as you could see.

The Shelby GT350H was the supercar built for the masses as well as for the Hertz Rent-A-Car company. This 1966 GT 350H lurks under a streetlight, waiting to take on the competition. The H model was a more humane version of the standard GT350, and the Hertz versions came with a back seat and a radio. One thousand were built and were rented to members of the Hertz Sports Car Club. Unfortunately, there is nothing like this at the airport rental lots nowadays.

The 1966 Shelby GT350H

Only in America are dreams for rent. To think you could get off an airline flight and slip behind the wheel of a race car. The Hertz rental car company introduced a legion of drivers to the Shelby firm. In the short term it probably cost Hertz money, but the exposure was incalculable.

Business was good for Shelby, but he was always on the lookout for sales opportunities. He found out that Hertz Rent-A-Car had a Hertz Sports Car Club, a program for high-end travelers with good driving records.

Chevrolet Corvettes were available, and Shelby wanted a piece of the action. He approached Peyton Cramer, who in turn met Hertz officials. On November 23, 1965, Hertz Rent-A-Car placed an order for 200 1966 GT350s, followed on December 21, 1966, for 800 more.

The color of the full-length stripe on the Shelby GT350H was Bronze Metallic. Here it covers the functional hood scoop, which also provided clearance between the air cleaner and the hood.

Like its Ford cousin, the Shelby Mustang retained the timeless first-generation fastback lines. Ford established the long hood/short deck body theme that would be reflected in all the future pony and musclecars.

The Magnum 500 was recognized as the factory Ford wheel to have. These durable wheels were made of steel and measured 14 by 6 inches. Surrounded by 6.95x14 Goodyear Blue Streak tires, the bias-ply tires were state of the art for the era.

Unlike the vents on the 1965 Shelby GT350, the 1966 model used a Plexiglas window installed in C-pillars to help overcome the large blind spot. The crisp lines of the Mustang design are seen here, the roof gracefully flowing into the deck surface.

The Hertz order eventually accounted for about 40 percent of Shelby's 1966 production.

The GT350Hs were mildly modified Shelby production vehicles. Unlike regular GT350s, the Hertz cars came with a back seat and radio. The first 85 units were equipped with four-speeds, and the rest were fitted with automatics. Shelby's auto-box had a different carburetor, and the manual transmission models were equipped with the Autolite 460 model. Most of them came black with gold stripes, but various other colors were used in the production run. This included white, red, blue, and green. All were adorned with the twin racing stripes. Interiors could be any color desired, as long as that desire was for black.

Under the hood lurked your standard Shelby-modified 289-ci screamer. Horsepower was still 306 at 6,000 rpm, and torque remained unchanged at 329 foot-pounds at 4,200 revs. All the standard Shelby mods were left intact, such as functional rear brake cooling ducts and the Monte Carlo bar across the engine compartment. The brakes, complete with competition metallic pads

and linings, were also retained from the regular production GT350s. The brakes had to be warmed in order to function properly, and unfortunately many customers found that the cold brakes didn't work. Too often, the H's front-end sheet metal acted as a brake as the car contacted an object. First boosters were installed and then softer brake materials were added. Covering the brakes were chrome-plated steel wheels, 14 -by-6-inch Magnum 500s manufactured by the Motor Wheel Corporation. Ground contact was maintained using 6.95x14 Goodyear Blue Streak tires.

Rental cars being rental cars, I suspect that GT350Hs were driven with a touch more enthusiasm than, oh say, a Nova. In 1968 and 1969, Hertz rented current Shelbys again, but without the "H" graphic on the side and with a bit less fanfare. The program worked. Hertz raised its profile in the battle with Avis, and Shelby sold a pack of cars. In these litigious times, it's hard to believe that anyone over 25 with a good record could slap down $17 a day and pay 17 cents a mile to drive a supercar down the road.

In the ever-growing horsepower war, Ford responded with the 1967 Mustang GTA, a 325-horsepower 390-ci V-8 mated to an automatic transmission. The tiny A behind the GT label on the rocker panel denoted that this 390-ci Mustang was equipped with an automatic transmission.

The Arrival of Big-Block High-Performance

Detroit has a habit of bringing out a new vehicle, lithe and trim, then adding mass in the name of public desire. Ford realized that the Mustang needed to grow to meet the increasing competition. General Motors was about to release the new Camaro/Firebird. The Pontiac GTO was building a cult following. Plymouth's Barracuda was improving. Ford realized its rivals were going to be installing big-block engines, and Ford was not going to be left behind in the horsepower wars.

The Mustang was the logical recipient of the FE-series big-block engines in FoMoCo's stable. The problem was the 390-ci engine wouldn't fit between the front suspension of the first-generation Mustang. The new model Mustang rode on the same wheelbase as the original—108 inches. But every other dimension grew. Overall length increased 2.0 inches to 183.6, while the width increased 2.7 inches to 70.9. Wheel track, the distance between same axle

wheels, grew 2.0 inches. This opened up room in the engine compartment.

These changes turned the Mustang from a nimble sports coupe into more of a Grand Touring car. The public loved it. While overall sales fell from 1966 levels, the 472,121 units sold kept the Mustang in the black and filling garages. These were the years when Total Performance ramped up to unbelievable levels.

The 1967 Mustang GT390

Buyers wanting a fire-breathing Mustang for model year 1967 had more choices. The Hi-Po 271-horsepower 289 V-8 was a strong, flexible powerplant and was still available for $433.55. The relatively lightweight mill helped the vehicle maintain cornering agility. But only 472 such engines were ordered for the car because most buyers were searching for tire-melting performance. So they opted for the "Thunderbird Special," a 390-ci iron block mill that delivered more brutish power for less money. For only $263.71, the customer got 320 ponies and 427 foot-pounds of torque under the long hood. Fitted with this

The 390 GT was Ford's big-block challenger for 1967. Due to the weight of the big-block engine, the car performed admirably in a straight line but was not a serious canyon carver.

engine and a comfortable amount of optional equipment, the price tag was in the vicinity of $4,100.

The widened track and front suspension modifications made room for the full-sized powerplant. The lower A-arm was lengthened 2.5 inches, while the upper A-arm pivot point was lowered. Not only was there room for the engine itself, but the cast-iron exhaust manifolds, as well as the growing slate of power options, required that extra space. Air conditioning, power steering, and power brakes, as well a score of interior options, pushed the Mustang into GT territory. On the test track, the original Pony Car delivered impressive numbers. In the January 1967 issue of *Car Life*, a 390 Mustang, equipped with a 3.25:1 rear axle ratio, recorded a quarter-mile

time of 15.5 seconds at 91.4 miles per hour. Eric Dahlquist of *Hot Rod* Magazine took a 390 2+2 to the drag strip and posted a time of 15.31 seconds at 93.45 miles per hour. The single 600-cfm Holley carburetor was bolted to a cast-iron intake manifold, with primary and secondary passages identical at 1.562 inches. At the

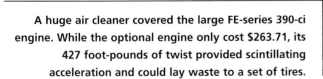

A huge air cleaner covered the large FE-series 390-ci engine. While the optional engine only cost $263.71, its 427 foot-pounds of twist provided scintillating acceleration and could lay waste to a set of tires.

Fog lamps mounted in the grille were for GTs only. The extractor scoops on the hood were for show only. Simulated brake cooling vents in front of the rear tires were a feature on the 1967 models.

other end of the power generation cycle were dual exhausts, standard on the GT.

Car Life registered a top speed of 113 miles per hour. With 11.38-inch-diameter Kelsey-Hayes front brake rotors and 10.00-inch rear drums, it took a while to bring a Mustang GT to a rapid halt. While the front/rear weight balance of 58/42 did not enhance handling, most big-block buyers were scarcely interested in navigating a tight twisty road.

With the increased size came increased weight. With the 390 under the hood, and a normal level of options, the 'Stang tipped the scale at 3,810 pounds. Straight-line stability was improved from the 1966 model and part of the reason was the Firestone Super Sport Wide Oval tires. The F70x14 rubber was praised by testers of the day, some of them preferring the Firestones to the radials then on the market. But the power steering communicated little road feel. With 3.6 turns lock to lock, and a turning diameter of 37.2 feet, the Mustang was not going to be confused with a true sports car, but it was Ford's new weapon in its battle against the new pony car entries. It paved the way, forever increasing cubic inches and wheelbases. And it whetted the appetites of young buyers, who were anxious to drive a vehicle unlike anything driven by their parents. Funny thing, kids of all ages loved the power. Still do.

Mustang styling significantly changed in 1967. The car's new styling cues included a more rakish appearance below the beltline and a revised grille. The 1967 model retained the three vertical taillight design, but the panel between the lights was now concave. High-performance models featured a chrome strip on the edge of the trunk lid. The dual exhaust was not only for show; a 390-ci engine needs to breathe.

With displacement increasing across the gamut of musclecars, it would only be a matter of time before a big-block Shelby was offered. The first 428-ci GT500 was released in 1967. The following year Shelby took the incredibly fast GT500 and made it faster by offering an even more exclusive GT500 KR. The KR moniker stood for "King of the Road," and in actuality

few musclecars could challenge it for street supremacy. The standard engine pumped out 335 horsepower while the KR engine produced a whopping 400 horsepower.

The 1967 Shelby GT500

When Ford increased the dimensions of the Mustang in 1967, Shelby had no choice but to change as well. The first-generation Shelbys were bred to dominate in the SCCA's B-Production class and found that the new market for sport racers favored cubic inches. For 1967, Shelby still offered the GT350, complete with the 306-horsepower, 289-ci small block. The increased size of the engine compartment allowed Shelby to shoehorn a much larger engine into it—the 428-ci V-8. It was called the GT500, if for no other reason than the number was larger than that of the competition. Some 47 were sold with the famed 427-ci side-oiler engine, but this engine was difficult to drive on the street. This powerplant was in its element at the racetrack. One such engine was installed in the GT500 and was driven by Carroll Shelby for tire testing. This "Super Snake" dynoed at close to 500 horsepower and could reach the upper end of 170 miles per hour.

But for street driving, the vast majority of the 2,048 GT500s built came with the hydraulic lifter–equipped 428-ci engine, rated at 355 horsepower at 5,400 rpm. Tire-smoking torque was listed at 420 foot-pounds at 3,200 revs, which was enough to quickly waste the Goodyear Speedway 350 E70x15 rubber. The cast-iron block had a 10.5:1 compression ratio and a bore and stroke of 4.13 x 3.98 inches. A "Police Interceptor" cam was installed, and an aluminum medium-rise dual-plane intake manifold, topped with a pair of Holley 650-cfm four-barrel carburetors (Model R-2804 in front and R-2805 in rear) and a progressive linkage handled fuel induction.

Inside the engine, the crankshaft and pistons were cast items, but the connecting rods were forged. *Car and Driver* magazine flogged one in the February 1967 issue, and the results were indicative of the big-hammer musclecar approach. From 0 to 60 took 6.5 seconds, and the quarter-mile was attacked in 15.0 seconds at 95 miles per hour. Their test vehicle was equipped with the optional $50 C-6 Cruise-O-Matic three-speed automatic transmission and a 3.50:1 rear axle ratio, for a top speed of 128 miles per hour at 5,400 rpm. This showed that the vehicle was leaning toward boulevard cruising, unlike the GT350's road racing bent.

The Shelby Mustangs carried some of the most graceful and elegant lines of any car offered during the musclecar era. The wide taillights were lifted from the Mercury Cougar and gave the big Shelby a distinctive look. Functional dual exhausts and a center-mounted gas cap helped give the GT500 KR a sporty look, as if it needed the help. The GT500 KR convertible listed for $4,594.

The front/rear weight distribution of 56.4/43.6 percent did little for carving corners, but weight transfer under heavy acceleration was impressive. The large engine added 176 pounds to the front tires, not what a road racing car needed. Speaking of heft, the GT500 tipped the scales at 3,370 pounds, and the $4,195 price tag was within a couple of hundred dollars of a big-block Corvette.

Like the Chevrolet sports car, fiberglass was used in the body, though the Shelby GT500 used fiberglass stylistic and aerodynamic bolt-on pieces, such as the extended nose, air scoops, and spoilers. The first batch of cars put the high beam headlights in the center of the grille, a strong styling statement that ran afoul of the California Department of Motor Vehicles regulation regarding the spacing of the lights. After the first 20 production cars were manufactured, the lamps were moved to the outside edges of the grille, predating the 1969 production Mustang. The relocated headlights helped increase airflow to the radiator and helped in cooling the sizable engine. The engine also had to supply power to such mandatory options as power brakes and steering, and the popular $356.09 air conditioning option. The pounds were adding up, and the focus was changing. Pure racing was out. Grand Touring was in. The GT500 was just a reflection of the time.

These handsome 10-spoke, 15-inch cast-aluminum wheels are collector's items today. The cobra emblem on the center cap is the same used on today's Cobra model.

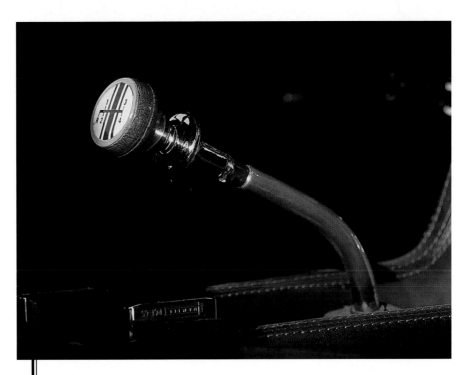

Shelby has never been shy about promotion, and placing his company colors on the shift knob was no surprise. It does make for a great-looking piece of hardware. The bent shape was reminiscent of the original Cobra's shifter.

The rubber seal on top of the air cleaner mated up to the bottom of the hood, and the scoops fed cool, outside air to the Cobra-Jet 428-ci engine. The huge engine was shoehorned into the engine bay; notice the tight fit between the valve covers and the shock towers.

The 1968¹/₂ 428 Cobra Jet

It was no April Fool. Introduced on April 1, 1968, an FE-based big block was slipped between the strengthened front shock towers to help the Mustang compete in the ever hotter muscle arena. The Camaro, Firebird, AMX, GTO, and Barracuda were grabbing headlines and customers from Ford. The pieces for a leading-class vehicle were on the shelf, but until the Cobra Jet was released, the Mustang found itself falling behind the competition. All that changed in April.

In the mid-1960s, the nation's number one Ford dealer was Robert Tasca, in East Providence, Rhode Island. A fan of motorsports, he had sponsored a long list of winning drag-race cars. But he was less than satisfied with the power output from the high-performance production Mustangs. After an employee burned down a 390-engined GT coupe one evening, the dealership

cobbled together a big-block engine, using a 428 Police Interceptor short block and a pair of 427 low-riser heads. A GTA 390 hydraulic cam and a 735-cfm Holley carburetor were installed as well. The hybrid creation ran the quarter-mile at 13.39 seconds at 105 miles per hour.

This vehicle got good press, and good press was not wasted on Ford. Quickly, the engineering team at Ford built the Cobra Jet engine, using parts on the shelves. They started with a 428 block that was recast in a nodular iron alloy, with more material in the ribbing. For cost considerations, two-bolt main bearings were retained, but this was not going to be a "racing" engine, so two bolts held the meaty connecting rods. The cast-aluminum piston helped get the 10.6:1 compression ratio needed to develop 335 horsepower at 5,600 rpm. The heads were 427 items, the 2.06-inch intake valves and 1.625-inch exhaust valves working to

Released in 1967, the 428-ci Cobra Jet was a mixture of off-the-shelf parts that resulted in a strong engine. In standard Ford dress, the 428 Cobra Jet produced 335 horsepower. The 428 in the KR was fitted with larger heads, oversized intake manifold, and a Holley 735 carburetor, and that helped the engine pump out 400 horsepower. *Randy Leffingwell*

The Cobra Jet option was an excellent way to suck in a racer, then promptly blow his doors off. The wheels saw widespread use in 1969 with the next generation of Mustangs. The Cobra Jet was only available in the coupe body style. *Randy Leffingwell*

produce 445 foot-pounds at 3,400 revs, enough to merge into most traffic.

Sitting on the aluminum intake manifold was a single 735-cfm Holley four-barrel carburetor. The camshaft was lifted from the 390 GT, with lift specs of 0.481/0.490 (intake/exhaust), while duration was 290 degrees.

From the outside, it didn't scream performance. The 428 Cobra Jet option meant that the Mustang was a GT, period. But any of the three body types—coupe, fastback, or convertible—could get the big-block engine. The functional hood scoop was tasteful yet sedate, and the stripe running the length of the hood a nod to performance past. A narrow side stripe looped

Chrome valve cleaners and an aluminum intake manifold hint at the tone that the 428-ci Cobra Jet engine took. Under the huge air cleaner was a single 735-cc Holley carburetor. This package generated an impressive 445 foot-pounds of torque. *Randy Leffingwell*

around the rear quarter scoop, and GT wheels completed the external package. Under the sheet metal, a number of mandatory options helped maintain control, such as the front power 11.38-inch disc brakes and the aforementioned braced front shock towers. Staggered rear shocks accompanied the four-speed CJ. The right side shock mounted in front of the rear axle in an attempt to reduce axle hop under heavy acceleration. A 31-spline axle was installed to minimize breakage, while the 9-inch rear end could be filled with 3.50:1, 3.91:1, or 4.30:1 gears. It all worked wonderfully together to produce a package that could only come from Detroit.

So what kind of bragging rights did $434 buy? Big ones. The March 1968 issue of *Hot Rod* magazine reported that Eric Dahlquist drove a 3.89:1 limited-slip, rear-axle ratio–equipped one down a drag strip in 13.56 seconds, crossing the finish line at 106.64 miles per hour. This wasn't bad for a four-seater weighing 3,240 pounds. The car bolted from 0 to 60 in 5.9 seconds, which topped the Shelby GT500's time of 6.2 seconds. The Goodyear Polyglas Wide-Oval tires never stood a chance. This was the beginning of sheer brute power, reasonably priced. You had to be a fool to run against one.

In case the occupants didn't notice the exterior graphics, the script in the center of the dash let everyone know that this was not a grocery-getter Mustang. The T-handle on the shifter was connected to the automatic transmission. *Randy Leffingwell*

Ultimate Muscle and the Generation After

The barbarians were at the gate. Hell, they ran it over. The vehicles that were rolling off of the production lines could only be called stupidly fast. Power output was rising faster than a Saturn V rocket, and many street cars exceeded the performance of pure race cars built only a couple of years before. Yet the push was on to raise the bar even higher.

Sales of selected models were directly related to competition, and vice versa. The battle between cross-town rivals Ford and Chevrolet was glowing white-hot, and the public could enjoy the fallout by signing on the dotted line. Even popular slang of the day found its way onto the side of automobiles. The vehicles had what it took under the hood, and they looked the part. There was no shortage of sizzle. It was applied with a broad brush, the more outrageous looking the better. These were wild times, and the Mustang was front and center in the pursuit of happiness. If you couldn't move faster than the speed of sound, at least you could be the Boss.

By 1971 the writing was on the wall. Pressure from the insurance industry and government-mandated emissions restrictions spelled doom for the musclecar. The fastback sports-roof Mustang was offered until 1973, albeit with serious softened compression ratios and reduced horsepower output. In an attempt to adjust to the new world order, Ford released the Mustang II in 1974. Starting with a 1971 Pinto chassis, the engineers massaged the platform to deliver what Lee Iacocca wanted in the next generation Mustang—a small, luxurious vehicle that delivered sporting fun at a reasonable price. It was a foot shorter than the original 1965 Mustang, and when ordered with the optional Ghia luxury package it contained more insulating material than the Lincoln Continental.

Sales were soft, to the tune of only 18,000 Mustang IIs hitting the street in the first month. But things changed the next month when OPEC turned off the oil wells. Suddenly the diminutive pony car was "the right car at the right time." By 1978 a low-production, high-performance Mustang was offered. It was called the King Cobra.

The Boss 302 was built to homologate the racing version, actively raced in the famed SCCA Trans-Am

The 1969 Boss 302

Whoever said racing improved the breed could use the Boss 302 as its poster car. In 1968, Ford found itself in a position of needing to build the Boss 302. Actually, Ford needed a production car to counter the Chevrolet

series. It wasn't a mere musclecar; it was a supercar. Fitted with a high-tech 290-horsepower 302 small block and equipped with critical suspension upgrades, the Boss was brutally fast and handled superbly.

Camaro Z/28 on the racetrack. The Dearborn firm was up to its axles in fighting for wins in the SCCA Trans-Am series. Ford had won the prestigious series in 1966 and 1967, but Chevrolet took home the trophy and the bragging rights in 1968. This just wouldn't do at Ford.

The Tunnel Port 302 engine had come up short, so engineering set about developing an engine that would level the playing field on the back straight at Riverside Raceway in California. Their efforts coincided with the arrival of a walking dynamo.

The Boss 302 was one of the most visually exciting Mustangs to ever turn a wheel. The adjustable wing on the trunk grabbed attention, and so did the rear widow louvers or sport slats. The slats sat on hinges at their front edge, and could be lifted up to gain access to the rear window for cleaning.

Semon "Bunkie" Knudsen been very influential at Chevrolet, a staunch believer of "Winning on Sunday, Selling on Monday." In 1968 he went to Ford and started revving up the company's profile on the track. Bunkie knew of the Z/28 and knew that Ford would get its clock cleaned unless an agile, strong racer in the mold of the mid-1960s Shelby GT350 was developed. SCCA rules required that at least 1,000 of the production version would be built, a challenge that Ford was more than willing to meet.

Knudsen got the ball rolling, but another former Chevrolet employee was instrumental in styling and naming of the new model. Larry Shinoda, designer of the famed 1963 Sting Ray and Mako Shark show cars, made the move to the Blue Oval in mid-May 1968. He, like Bunkie, knew that the youth market was interested in vehicles that could frighten the center stripes off the surface of a curvy road. Shinoda had his finger on the pulse of America's kids, and he forwarded the slang phrase "Boss" to the boardroom for consideration on the sport version of the newly expanded, again, Mustang. The execs gave a collective thumbs down, but Bunkie got it—and he saw that the rest of upper management got it too.

The green light was finally given for Shinoda's design, including the large front and rear spoilers, rear window slats, and bold paint and tape graphics.

Besides, Bunkie liked to win, both on and off the track. So no small amount of engineering effort was spent to make both the street and track versions of the Boss 302 first in wins and sales. While Kar Kraft built the 450-horsepower racers, the street copy was rolled down the standard assembly line, slowly being fitted with enough mechanical improvements to turn the pony car into arguably the best Mustang built during the musclecar era.

During the 1968 Trans-Am season, Ford ran the Tunnel Port 302, a race-only engine that had a propensity for prematurely expiring. Okay, it would croak before the checkered flag flew. For the 1969 season, things would be different. First, Ford actually built the required 1,000 street-version cars. Second, while the engine still displaced 302 ci, that was about all it shared with its troublesome predecessor.

Ford started with a four-bolt main bearing block, the C8. It was part of the Windsor family of engines. Later in the 1969 production run, C9 or DO castings were used, but the basic configuration remained the same. Bore and stroke was 4.0 by 3.0 inches. Almost all of the entire reciprocating mass was of forged construction. The crankshaft was cross-drilled forged steel, the forged connecting rods used 3/8-inch bolts, and the forged aluminum domed pistons used 5/64-inch compression rings and 3/16-inch oil rings.

The "Boss" heads were lifted from the new 351 Cleveland engine. This was the single largest contributor to the performance that was unleashed. The heads were found to have the same bolt-hole pattern and bore spacing as the block. T-valve ports within these heads were large enough to swallow common household pets. Canted to produce a polyangular combustion chamber, the 1.71-inch exhaust valve looked puny next to the 2.23-inch intake. The valves were tilted to allow tremendous gas flow at both low and high engine speeds, especially high. The rocker arms sat on screw-in studs, and pushrod guide plates kept the valves pointed in the correct direction during tach testing engine speeds. The mechanical camshaft had a duration of 290 degrees for both intake and exhaust valves and an overlap of 58 degrees. Valve lift was considerable at .477 inch. The intake ports measured 2.4 by 1.7 inches and were attached to an aluminum high-rise intake manifold.

A 780-cfm Holley carburetor resided on top of the special manifold. That was a tip-off that this engine was built for more than hauling groceries. With 1.68-inch-

Former Chevrolet stylist Larry Shinoda was responsible for the Boss's appearance. He designed the Boss 302 graphic package and deleted the nonfunctional rear quarter brake ducts. The same graphics package was used on the Trans-Am Boss 302 race cars, which added to the allure of this illustrious car. In 1969 the Boss 302 option set a buyer back $3,788. Today, a low-mileage, unmolested example will typically fetch $20,000 or more.

To extract maximum power and reliability, Ford put its engineering might behind the Boss 302 engine. The 290-horsepower small block featured large heads with massive valve ports, four-bolt main bearing caps, aluminum windage tray, forged steel connecting rods and crank, forged aluminum pistons, and a massive Holley 780 carburetor. Peak power was made at 5,800 rpm, enough to run the quarter-mile in less than 15 seconds. With the 4.3 Detroit Locker rear end, the Boss galloped from 0 to 60 miles per hour in 5.5 seconds.

diameter primaries and secondaries, this manual choke monster could pass enough fuel to allow the driver to watch the gas gauge move.

Needless to say, with its 10.5:1 compression, it was imperative that the owner use premium fuel. The spec sheet said 290 horsepower at 5,800 rpm and 290 foot-pounds of torque at 4,300 revs. To keep from showering the street with hot, oily engine parts, Ford installed a rev limiter, designed to randomly short out cylinders at 6,150 rpm. Street engines typically didn't need to spin that fast to reach maximum power; however, race engines were a different matter.

Getting the power to the ground was the job of the modified suspension. The front end used high-rate (350-pound) springs and Gabriel shock absorbers. A .72-inch stabilizer bar was installed to minimize body lean under hard cornering. In the rear, the familiar live axle held heavy-duty 31 spline axles. Leaf springs (150-pound) and staggered Gabriel shocks tried to hold axle hop to a minimum when getting heavy into the throttle. But pushing the right pedal was *fun!*

In the September issue of *Car Life*, a Boss 302 was put through its paces. The quarter-mile was run in 14.85 seconds at 96.15 miles per hour. The folks at *Car and Driver* (June 1969) put the whip to the Boss, coming up with a drag strip performance of 14.57 seconds at 97.57 miles per hour. While the numbers tell a tale, it's only part of the story.

This was a Mustang built to turn as well as go fast in a straight line. The desire to best the Bowtie crew resulted in a fine road car. Shod with 15.0 by 7.0-inch Goodyear F60x15 Polyglas rubber on Magnum wheels, and a 55.7/44.3-front/rear-weight balance, the Boss 302 navigated turns with the best of them. Because of the 7.0-inch rims, the fenders had to have modified wheel openings to clear the tires. With the rim width, the front spindles had to be replaced with units having larger wheel bearings. Told you Ford was serious about getting the Boss to run.

If you wanted an automatic transmission, well, too bad. A wide-ratio four-speed top-loader manual box, with a 2.78 first gear handled gear changes, while a 3.50:1 rear axle ratio was on the other end of the driveshaft. A close-ratio gearbox with a 2.32 first gear was available, however.

This much excitement didn't come cheap: A normally equipped Boss 302 went for about $3,788, while the standard Mustang SportsRoof went for about $2,618. Money well spent? Oh yes. Ford built 1,628 Boss 302s in 1969, and news of the vehicle got out to the tune of 7,013 in 1970, the last year of Boss 302 production. Was it worth it to Ford? Oh yes. While the Camaro won the Trans-Am title in 1969, the Blue Oval was finally victorious in 1970, the Boss 302 bringing home the trophy.

Bunkie was a happy man, and the Mustang mystique was burnished just a little bit brighter.

The graceful 15-by-7.0-inch Magnum rims required gently flaring the wheel arches to gain sufficient tire clearance. Suspension enhancements included oversized front spindles, shock tower braces, large front sway bar, staggered high-performance shocks, front disc brakes, and 16:1 steering ratio.

By 1969, America had reached the height of the horsepower wars. The 1969 Mach 1 was Ford's chosen weapon. Available with a 351, 390, or 428 V-8, there was a powerplant option to suit every driver. The Mach 1 featured the

timeless "SportsRoof" fastback body profile, a classy styling package, and a suspension similar to the Boss 302.

The 1969 Mach 1 428 Cobra Jet

Image is powerful. The Mustang was definitely about image. Ever since Job 1 rolled down the assembly line, the original pony car projected an aura of youth and excitement. Buyers wanting a healthy dose of verve could order any number of sporty versions, culminating in mid-1968 in the Cobra Jet–equipped GT. But the styling was starting to look a bit dated. The Mustang's competitors were rolling out fresh sheet metal, and the resulting sales put pressure on Ford to restore the 'Stang to the head of the pack. So in the finest Detroit fashion, the Mustang grew again. While the wheelbase stayed the same at 108 inches, overall vehicle length grew 3.8 inches, all of it in the front.

When the Mach 1 option debuted in 1969, it was a well-balanced, sporting Grand Touring vehicle. Available only with the SportsRoof (fastback) model, the replacement for the GT came with plenty of flash, and when properly optioned, plenty of fast. As a kind of high-powered boulevard cruiser, Ford fitted the Mach 1 with 55 pounds of insulation. While the Mach 1 was Ford's top high-performance SportsRoof Mustang, it could be fitted with the machinery needed to put a smile on a tire salesman's face. That machinery was called the 428 Cobra Jet.

The styling of the 1969 Mach 1 garnered compliments from all quarters. The aggressive front end was fitted with four headlights, the only year that Mustangs would be so equipped. Vehicles destined to break the speed of sound came with hood pins as standard, but they could be left off. The vents that had been found on the side of the car in front of the rear wheels were now moved to the area just below the rear quarter windows. Still, they stressed form over function.

At the rear, the concave panel was still flanked by three vertical tail lamp lenses, and the small tail spoiler gave the Mach 1 a Trans-Am look, if not quite the performance. The lower body stripe was made of reflective tape that glowed at night when headlights struck it. The interior was decked out with high-back seats covered in "Comfortweave," genuine simulated teak wood appliqué by the acre, and basic instrumentation. A console ran down the center of the interior, and a large clock faced the passenger, no doubt ready for the next rally. Depressing a rubber strip that ran the circumference of the steering wheel activated the Rim-Blow steering wheel's horn. The view over the hood was spectacular, the sound track thrilling, and the thrust was ready and on cue.

Under the long hood was one of three engines. The standard Mach 1 mill was the 351-ci Windsor, topped with a two-barrel carburetor and making all of 250 horsepower. Next up the 351-ci ladder was the four-barrel carbureted version helping to generate 290 horsepower. But for those who wanted something with presence, the 428 Cobra Jet was top dog. This was essentially the same engine offered in the 1968 Mustang, same 10.6:1 compression, same huge single four-barrel carb, same 335 rated horsepower. This engine could be installed in any of the three body models of Mustang, but when installed in the Mach 1, well, it was a match made in *gearhead* heaven.

The 428 Cobra Jet was basically a drag racing engine in search of a fight. With the 428 big block holding the front tires down, the front/rear weight distribution of 59.3/40.7 meant that the Boss 302 driver would not need to worry on a twisty road. But the Mach 1 was about styling, about exuding a menacing presence. With the stock 14-inch Goodyear Polyglas tires on 6-inch rims, the brutal torque, 440 foot-pounds (3,400 rpm) worth, could—and would—overpower the rubber contact patches.

Ordering the Cobra Jet option put the "Competition Handling" suspension under the 3,607-pound musclecar. This included higher rate front and rear springs, a stiff anti-sway bar, and staggered rear shocks when the four-speed manual transmission was installed. The power brakes featured single-piston caliper front discs, and rear drums were an option that made sense with that much iron in the lead. Even so, brake performance was less than stellar, *Car and Driver* halting a 428 Mach 1 in 256 feet from 80 miles per hour.

But the Mach 1 was not built to stop. It was made to rear its nose in the air and howl down a stretch of pavement. In a January 1969 test by the *Popular Hot Rodding* crew, a Cobra Jet Mach 1 flew down the quarter-mile in 13.69 seconds at 103.44 miles per hour with an automatic transmission. The scribes at *Car and Driver* didn't make it to the finish line at such a pace; 14.3 seconds showed on the clock, while the speedometer read 100 miles per hour over the finish line. Their vehicle, using an automatic and 3.91:1 gears in the rear axle, generated a top speed of 115 miles per hour. The midrange torque was quite impressive, with a firm push from 40 to 80 miles per hour. Under heavy acceleration, the suspension predictably squatted and the driver's compartment was filled with the sound of a throaty, howling big-block V-8. It was an image that Detroit fostered, and the reality was even better than the dream.

Equipped with air conditioning, power steering, and other comfort features, the 335-horsepower 428-ci engine still had enough power to turn quarter-mile times in the high 14-second range. The Shaker hood was a popular option, allowing the world to watch as the engine shook as the accelerator was depressed.

The tilt steering wheel swings away to allow easy entry. Squeezing the gasket that ran the circumference of the steering activated the horn. Genuine wood-grain appliqué added warmth to the interior, while the Comfortweave upholstery covered the seats, and a large clock faced the front seat passenger.

Simulated rear brake–cooling ducts were fitted to the area below the rear side windows. The flat black finish on the hood reduced reflections, and the hood pins were a nice high-performance touch.

The Torino Talladega was Ford's secret weapon in stock car racing competition during 1969. Aerodynamic principles were being effectively applied in NASCAR, and Ford had to compete against the winged Dodge Daytona Charger. The Talladega featured an aerodynamically sculpted nose extension and front bumper.

1969 Ford Torino Talladega

As the 1968 NASCAR season drew to a close, word of Dodge's secret weapon, the aerodynamic Charger 500, had already gotten out—and the competition was scared. Charger was already a fierce competitor, thanks largely to the Hemi engine. A sleek body would only make the Charger that much tougher to beat.

Upset that Chrysler wouldn't let him drive a Charger 500, long-time Plymouth driver and NASCAR superstar Richard Petty went shopping for a new ride. He wasn't about to finish as an "also-ran."

While the street versions of the Talladega were powered by the 335-horsepower 428 Cobra Jet, the race versions typically carried Boss 429s.

Production Talladega interiors were only slightly more comfortable than their race car counterparts'. A bench seat and column shifter were standard.

Ford was only too anxious to bring Petty on board. And they had just the car to offer him: the new Torino Talladega, which had been created in response to the Charger 500. With the Torino Talladega's fastbacklike rear end and its extended front end—which tapered slightly and used a modified Fairlane rear bumper on its front end to slice through the wind more easily—Petty knew he had found a car with the right stuff to compete against the wind-cheating Chargers.

And compete it did. Petty won his first outing in a Ford, at Richmond, and took 8 more firsts that season behind the wheel of a Talladega, along with a number of close second- and third-place finishes. Still, Petty finished second in points, after fellow Talladega driver David Pearson, who racked up 11 wins and 31 other top-five finishes.

Interestingly, the street Talladegas weren't available with the thundering Boss 429 powerplant that powered Petty's and Pearson's NASCAR racers. Instead, civilian buyers had to settle for a 335-horsepower 428 Cobra Jet. But that substitution vastly improved the street-driving characteristics of the Talladega, since the Boss '9 was notorious for its cantankerous nature and need for frequent tuning. The 428-CJ, on the other hand, was docile and torquey, day after day.

There was little else about the Torino Talladega that was well suited to daily driving. Its extended nose added some 6 inches to the car's length and made it more difficult to drive, especially when attempting to park. And visibility out the gently sloped rear window was poor, due to large blind spots created by the massive C-pillars. And if that wasn't enough to deter most buyers, the bare-bones interior made few friends. The Torino Talladega was built for speed, not comfort. If a part didn't help the Talladega go faster, it wasn't available on the car.

The "no-frills" mentality even carried over to the exterior identification of the car. Unlike its Mercury sibling, the Cyclone Spoiler II, which featured bold red and white or blue and white paint highlighted by either "Dan Gurney Special" or "Cale Yarborough Special" decals, the Talladega was available in traditional Torino colors with only three small "T" emblems to identify it—one on the top of each door, and another on the gas cap.

Despite the Talladega's regular visits to Victory Lane, it wasn't tremendously popular with the buying public. NASCAR rules dictated that Ford had to sell at least 500 copies of the Talladega for the car to be legal for competition; at year's end, only 754 Talladegas had been assembled (plus an estimated 519 copies of the similar Spoiler II Mercury).

Still, the very fact that Ford went to such great lengths to create a car capable of dominating NASCAR racing makes the 1969 Torino Talladega a memorable piece of musclecar history.

The 1969 Boss 429

If the Boss 302 was a rapier, the Boss 429 was a broadsword. A tool built to cut a wide swath in NASCAR competition, but it also successfully competed in NHRA and AHRA stock classes. This monster never would have seen the street if it had not been for the racing regulations that called for the engine to be available to the public. Yet Ford was deep into competing with the rest of Detroit on Sunday. The Chrysler Hemi and Chevrolet's Rat engines were kicking ass and taking names, and Ford wasn't going to be left as the perennial runner-up.

Ford needed a new race engine for the Torino Talladega and Mercury Cyclone. Marketing was convinced that it would be a lot easier selling a high-powered Mustang to the public than a big-block intermediate. An agreement was reached with NASCAR officials in which Ford had to install at least 500 new engines in the Boss 429 in order for the engine to be in race versions of the Cyclones and Talledegas.

Enter the "385" family of engines. Introduced in 1968, this thin-wall design engine, in 429- and 460-ci incarnations, saw duty in the Thunderbird and Lincolns. The Ford engineers didn't cook up a low-revving luxury cruiser engine, however. This was a racing engine. Basic block architecture was passenger-car 429, but it was cast from nodular iron. The heads differed in almost every possible respect from the standard 429.

They were made from aluminum, in an attempt to hold weight down. The 429-ci engine with prototype iron heads weighed in at more than 900 pounds. The alloy heads used a valvetrain arrangement that saw the valve stems going in apparently random directions. In fact, the combustion chambers were semi hemispherical. The nickname "twisted Hemi" came from the valve angle, and "Blue Crescent" was derived from the Blue Oval and the shape of the chambers. The heads were sealed to the iron block using copper rings and O-rings instead of head gaskets. Inside the heads were massive valves, meant to put large amounts of racing fuel into contact with the forged aluminum pistons. The intake valves were 2.29 inches in diameter, and the valve seat cut at 30 degrees. The exhausts measured in at 1.91 inches, and the seats cut at 45 degrees. Valve lift was .440–inch, and duration was 296 degrees exhaust, 282 degrees intake, and was activated by a hydraulic camshaft.

The bore and stroke was 4.36 by 3.59 inches. Holley's 735-cfm four-barrel, model C9AF-9510-S, sat atop an aluminum intake manifold. The 10.5:1 compression

The Boss 429 is one of the best and certainly one of the most exclusive big-block Mustangs ever built. The Boss 429 was essentially a racing engine crammed into the tight confines of the 1969–1970 Mustang

helped to deliver a rated 375 horsepower at 5,200 rpm, and the torque rating of 410 foot-pounds arrived at 3,400 revs. The cross-drilled, forged crankshaft was attached to forged connecting rods. In fact, there were two versions of the Boss 429 engine, the S and T editions. The S engine sported NASCAR-grade connecting rods that used huge rod bolts that weighed almost 3 pounds each. The T engine had standard production con rods.

With such a huge engine, the Mustang was woefully short of room under the hood. Considerable modifications

SportsRoof. Like the Boss 302, the Boss 429 was created so Ford would comply with minimum build rules of NASCAR stock car racing. Although the 429 was a competent musclecar, it didn't realize its potential in stock form due to a mild cam and a small carburetor. When a Boss 429 engine was given an aggressive cam, a larger carburetor, and large headers, it could battle Hemis.

were needed to squeeze the detuned race motor into the pony car. There was no way that Ford could assemble the minimum 500 vehicles on the regular line, so the job was farmed out to Kar Kraft, Ford's quasi-official race shop in Brighton, Michigan. Ford would ship Mustang SportsRoof bodies that were meant to hold 428 SCJ engines. Kar Kraft widened the engine bay by moving the front shock towers outward, and relocated the suspension mounting points down and outward 1 inch. An export brace helped tie the cowl to the shock towers to retain strength. Due to

the tight confines under the hood with the enormous engine, the 85-amp battery was moved to the relatively spacious trunk. Air conditioning was not available because there was no room for the bulky components.

External modifications were rather low-key, a deep front spoiler and front fender decals. An enormous functional hood scoop sat on top of the hood, looking like it would be at home at Daytona. Chrome "Magnum 500" steel wheels were surrounded by Goodyear Polyglas F60x15 tires. The 7-inch rim width required fender

In order to fit the massive Boss 429 into the engine bay, a number of suspension modifications had to be carried out. The shock towers were revamped and the suspension mounting points were relocated. The 429 rode on Magnum 500 15-by-7-inch wheels, and like the Boss 302, the front spindles were massaged for strength and wheelwell clearance.

The huge hood scoop was functional and distinctive. Any engine as large as the Boss 429's needed a massive amount of fresh air. Its aggressive design complemented the fastback lines of the body.

modifications for tire clearance. Under the skin, the front spindles were beefed up, just like the Boss 302. The brakes were identical to those on the Boss 302, with power front disc and rear drums. Shock absorbers were heavy-duty Gabriel units, and the live rear axle contained standard 3.91:1 gears in a Traction-Lok differential.

Gear sets from 3.50:1 to a Detroit Locker 4.30:1 were available, depending on the desired acceleration rate. Because of the added weight over the front tires, a rear 0.62-inch anti-sway was installed to counter the effects of understeer. A 0.94-inch front bar worked to minimize body roll. After all, the big Boss 429 did have a front/rear weight distribution of 56/44.

And how did the Boss 429 perform on the street? Like an emasculated race car engine, which in street trim is essentially what it was. With the relatively small carburetor, mild camshaft, and rev limiter, the Boss 429 didn't conquer the competition like a Hemi-powered Mopar. It produced a less-than-spectacular 0 to 60 time of 7.1 seconds, while the drag strip was tackled in 14.9 seconds, with a trap speed of 102.85 miles per hour. The velocity at the finish line indicated that the Boss 429 was coming into the heart of its powerband at the end of the strip. Like most Hemi design engines, mid- and upper-range power was their forte. The Boss 429 was no different.

A 428 CJ Mach 1 would hold its own in most street contests with the Boss 429. If a larger carburetor, headers, and a more aggressive camshaft were fitted, however, the engine came alive, generating sinful amounts of power—power that was on par with Hemis and LS-6-powered cars. Then the broadsword would swoop down, smiting the infidels. In an age of large, the Boss 429 was a legend in its own time, and now.

The concave panel between the triple vertical taillights continued in the 1969 model year. The original dealer sticker used the Shelby Cobra design as its highly recognizable emblem.

On the interior side, the Boss 429 was nearly identical to its standard SportsRoof and less powerful brethren. The instruments were buried in deep tunnels in the dash and were easy to read.

The Boss 429 carried a simple straightforward styling package. A small outlined graphic on the front fender denoted that this was a Boss 429. Differing from the Boss 302, the 1969 429 carried fake brake duct scoops and C-pillar badges, but the rear deck spoiler was an option. The Boss 429 conversion was done at Kar Kraft, Ford's semi-official race shop. The engine was designed to compete on the tracks of NASCAR.

The massive Boss 429 was derived from the 385 series engines. Its features included O-rings instead of head gaskets to seal the heads to the block, semi-hemispherical combustion chambers, massive cylinder heads and mammoth ports, and four-bolt main bearing caps. Due to the tight fit in the engine compartment, power accessories were not installed, and the battery was installed in the trunk.

The Boss 302 and 429 were discontinued after 1970. With Ford no longer officially involved in racing, a high-performance 351 was given the Boss name. Although the Boss 351 was the last of the Boss line, it had superb handling and was an extremely fast musclecar. The small-block screamer could reach 60 miles per hour from a stop in less than 6 seconds, and it could cover the quarter-mile in the low 14s.

The 1971 Boss 351

The original pony car had grown to Clydesdale proportions. Ford was on a two-year styling cycle, and the Mustang was no exception. Growth in all directions was the norm. Detroit was living by the bigger-is-better creed. The wheelbase was stretched to 109 inches; the overall length increased 2.1 inches to 189.5 inches. Width was up 2.4 inches, and the average vehicle weight was 500 pounds more than that of the 1970 models. The Mustang was bulking up.

One of the reasons for the increased heft was the need to fit monster-sized powerplants between the front shock towers without heavily modifying the engine compartment. The 429-ci Cobra Jet was still on the option sheet for the last time, and the Boss 302 was absent in 1971. But the spirit of that capable road missile lived on for one more year in the Boss 351. Ford had stepped away from racing, which was the reason the Boss line of Mustangs was created in the first place. Ford announced its departure from competition two days before the Boss 351 debuted at the Detroit Auto Show.

From a dynamic standpoint, it was one of the most capable 'Stangs Ford had built to date. But the insurance companies had started to put serious pressure on the auto industry to build more socially responsible (milder) vehicles. In addition, the government-mandated emission standards were sucking the performance out of automobiles like a swarm of leeches. So inevitably the musclecar craze faded.

But the Mustang stepped away from the pulpit of speed in fine fashion. The formula of a high-revving, high-output small-block engine installed in a responsive chassis worked in the late 1960s, and it worked in 1971. A 351 Cleveland engine was the starting point, and the four-bolt main bearing caps provided stability on the bottom end. The bore and stroke of 4.0 by 3.5 inches gave the 351 engine the same bore as the Boss 302 and a 1/2-inch longer stroke. Extruded pop-up aluminum pistons were attached to magnafluxed forged connecting rods that attached to a Brinell-tested cast crankshaft. A pair of Boss 302 heads, featuring modified cooling passages, complete with 2.195-inch intake valves and 1.714-inch exhaust valves, sat on top of the cast-iron block. The poly-angle heads were built to flow well at high rpms. To this end, the mechanical camshaft was more radical than the previous Boss small block. Valve lift was a healthy .491 inch, while the duration of both intake and exhaust valves was 324 degrees.

Metering the fuel/air mixture was the responsibility of the 750-cfm Autolite Spread Bore four-barrel carburetor. The primaries were only 1.56 inches in diameter, the

This was the last year that the hood carried functional air scoops. Twist locks, giving a cleaner appearance, replaced pin hood locks. The argent-colored chin spoiler was susceptible to scrapes.

better to stretch mileage. But the 1.96-inch secondaries looked like a couple of manholes on top of the engine. An aggressive 11.0:1 compression allowed the engine to produce 330 horsepower at 5,400 rpm. The max torque of 370 foot-pounds was delivered at 4,000 rpm. An electronic rev limiter cut out spark to cylinders at 6,150 rpm. And the only transmission installed was the top-loader four-speed manual, complete with Hurst shifter.

The functional Ram-Air NACA ducts on the hood fed cool, dense air to the engine at speed. In the February 1971 issue of *Car and Driver*, the Boss 351 posted 14.1 seconds at 100.6 miles per hour. The all-important 0 to 60 miles per hour in 5.8 was nothing to sneeze at, even at the peak of the musclecar era. In the March 1971 issue of *Road Test*, the Boss 351 took 5.9 seconds to reach 60 miles per hour, on its way to covering the quarter-mile in 13.98 seconds, tripping the finish line lights at 104.1 miles per hour. Top speed was in the vicinity of 117 miles per hour, as off-the-line pull was favored over top speed. The Boss 351 had nothing to apologize for on the track.

The Boss 351 engine was based on the 351 Cleveland block that carried a cast-iron timing change cover. Other high-performance features included four-bolt main bearing caps, shot-peened connecting rods, forged pistons, and a solid lifter camshaft.

Like the Boss 302s that predated the 351, handling was not ignored. Also like the Boss 302s, the Competition Suspension was underneath, with high-rate front coil springs and 53-inch rear leafs. Staggered rear shocks were installed, as well as 11.3-inch front disc brake rotors and 10 by 2-inch rear drums. A front 7/8-inch and a rear 5/8-inch anti-sway bar helped reduce understeer.

Variable-ratio power steering was installed in a Mustang for the first time. *Car and Driver* had nothing but praise for it, saying, "Easily the most significant of the Mustang's mechanical advancements has been made in the steering. It's not particularly quick on center but it is remarkably precise—certainly as good as the best from Detroit—and small steering corrections can be easily and accurately made."

The dramatic styling was successful in turning heads. The long hood and short rear deck formula was in full flower. From behind the wheel, the hood looked like the flight deck of an aircraft carrier, while the rear window was only 14 degrees from horizontal. Bold side stripes and hood treatments left no doubt as to the purpose of the Boss 351, the massive front spoiler trying to hold the bow down at high speed. This Boss rode on F60x15 tires on Magnum 500 wheels. The front pair held up 58 percent of the vehicle's weight. Total poundage was 3,860, up more than 300 pounds over the Boss 302. The larger engine helped overcome the heft.

The price of the Boss 351 was hefty as well, with dealers asking $4,124 for the car before options were ladled on. This might be one of the reasons only 1,806 were sold, and another might be the rise in gasoline prices in 1971. For a vehicle that could only get 14 miles per gallon on a good day, cubic inches translated into cubic dollars at the gas station. The introduction of unleaded gasoline in 1972 did nothing for the future of performance. Thus, the Boss line of Mustangs was shown off of the stage. But the Boss 351 was the culmination of a line of streetable race cars that brought glory to Ford. And more than a few thrills to the lucky drivers.

Tape graphics were a popular and inexpensive way for a manufacturer to make a model stand out from the crowd during the musclecar era. The Boss 351 was a prime example, but unlike a couple of years later, the 1971 Boss 351 had the power to back the image.

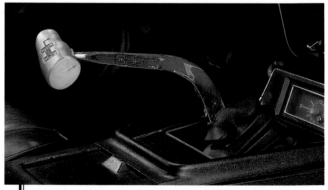

Like its predecessor, the Boss 351 was only available with a four-speed manual transmission. The stout Hurst shifter controlled the four-speed gearbox, making the rapid shifting a joy.

Known more for its luxury, cars such as the 1969 Cougar Eliminator showcased Mercury's muscle-building talents. Larry Shinoda, who styled the Boss 302, developed the Eliminator package for Mercury. The semi-fastback, side stripes, and deck lid spoiler gave it a unique look.

Mercury Division: Fast Fords with High Fashion

While Mercury's mission was to provide luxurious models at affordable prices, the company realized the importance of tapping into the burgeoning performance market. Apart from the additional sales and exposure, such a move would also help the company build brand loyalty among the young buyers in the hope of converting them into buyers of high-end (and highly profitable) luxury cars later in life.

Like its sister division, Ford, Mercury created a performance reputation the old-fashioned way: by racing—and winning. Battles took place on drag strips and stock car ovals around the country.

Mercury built a limited run of Comets aimed at dominating drag strip competitions. A 289-powered model was cleared for competition in NHRA's B/FX class, and Mercury covered the A/FX class with Comets stuffed full of high-riser and SOHC 427s. Drag racing legends Dyno Don Nicholson, Eddie Schartman, and Hayden Proffitt all lit up the win lights in Mercurys; Dyno Don even did it in a Mercury Comet station wagon, which he believed had better weight transfer characteristics than the standard sedan—something he credited for his 11-second class record and a season that saw only a single defeat.

And when it came to the NASCAR circuit, Comets—and later Cyclones—carried the Mercury name into Victory Lane. As the aero wars took center stage, Mercury was there with its Cyclone Spoiler and subsequent Cyclone Spoiler II.

Naturally, as word spread of Mercury's on-track accomplishments, its off-track business picked up, though never quite to levels that were completely commensurate with its finishes at the races. That meant that a significant portion of the buying public ended up missing out on the street versions of each of Mercury's racing models.

The buyers who didn't miss out were rewarded with cars that were every bit the equal of the more popular Ford performance models, but with more comfortable interiors and more stylized bodies. Mercury musclecars had the added advantage (for those buyers who valued it for some less-than-strictly-legal reasons) of not looking like musclecars nor did many people know much about their performance potential, so Mercury drivers had little trouble convincing unsuspecting victims to race them.

But when "performance" became a dirty word in the early 1970s, Mercury wisely refocused itself on the luxury car market. And though Mercury occasionally released performance cars throughout the remainder of the twentieth century—cars such as the imported Capri in the early 1970s, the 5.0-liter Mustang-based Capri of the 1980s, and the sporty Cougar at the turn of the century—its days of building musclecars were over. The surviving 1960s and 1970s Mercury musclecars have been left to preserve the memory of Mercury's hottest machines.

1969 Mercury Cougar Eliminator

An upscale Ford that's just right for taking down—or shaking down—the competition.

Despite all its market research, the various concept cars that were meant to test the waters, and the fact that the Mustang was going to be based on the Falcon underpinnings, the Mustang was still a huge financial risk for Ford Motor Company. Understandably, the company wasn't eager to let its Mercury division rush down a similar development path until the Mustang had proven itself.

Of course, following the sales stampede created by the 1965 Mustang debut in April 1964,

Cougar Eliminators were available with a variety of engines, including the Boss 302 and base 351, but this particular 1969 model carried the legendary 428 Cobra Jet. With dual exhaust and a shaker hood, the 335-horsepower 428-powered Eliminator was a monster on the street.

there was little reason to hold back on plans for a Mercury pony car. In the fall of 1966 the Cougar hit showrooms featuring a number of refinements that differentiated it from the Mustang and uniquely qualified it as a Mercury, including softer suspension calibrations, a 3-inch wheelbase stretch, and of course the unique front- and rear-end treatments and other bodywork changes.

Though hardly the instant success that the Mustang was, the Cougars sold well—over 100,000 units a year during the first few years. For 1969 the Cougar was restyled and an exciting new performance model joined the line-up: the Eliminator.

The Eliminator, like Pontiac's GTO Judge, combined outstanding performance and a high measure of luxury with an unmistakable and aggressive appearance. Performance-wise, the Eliminator picked up where the previous year's GT model left off. Ride and handling were dictated by the Competition Suspension package, which offered taut handling without a jarring ride. More important to race fans were the engines, transmissions, and rear axle assemblies that were available—and there were several.

The base Eliminator engine was the 290-horse 351-4V, which was optionally available on Cougars. Up a step from that was the marginally more powerful Marauder 390 at 320 horsepower, or the Boss 302 with its 290 horsepower. The Cobra Jet 428 that appeared in late 1968 remained available, and for a very brief time the Boss 429 could be ordered, but only if you had connections—just two found their way under Cougar hoods.

Buyers interested in a great driving car were wise to select the Boss 302, which was the very same high-winding engine that highlighted the Boss 302 Mustang. It was widely known that the Boss 302's 290 horsepower and equal torque ratings were greatly under-rated. Though a bit twitchy for around-town driving, the Boss 302—and, indeed, the Eliminator—was in its element blasting down twisting, curving roads.

On the other hand, buyers who were more into short jaunts of, say, a quarter-mile or so, were better served by the Cobra Jet 428. As with the Boss 302, the CJ's 335-horsepower rating was somewhat less than believable, especially given the durability built into the engine when delivered in Super Cobra Jet form, with its LeMans-style rods, heavy-duty crank, and other fortified components. The big-block 428

The Cougar's Mustang roots showed through inside, where the semi-cockpit-style instruments are obviously derived from the Mustang. A large analog tachometer and speedometer fed vital information to the pilot. Like other Ford products of the day, it featured the rim-blow steering wheel.

also made for an excellent street warrior, though it lacked the handling prowess that the smaller, lighter Boss 302 afforded.

As improved as the Eliminator was over a typical Mustang, and as competent as it was on the street and racetracks, it just never caught on with the public. Still, in spite of its May 8, 1969, intro date and little promotional fanfare, Mercury dealers had little trouble moving 2,411 copies of the Eliminator by the end of the 1969 model production in July. But a full year of production in 1970 actually saw a dip in sales to 2,200 units, with just under half getting the base 351 Cleveland engine and the other half split evenly between Boss 302 and 428CJ engines. Such low production numbers hardly justified the engineering, marketing, and sales efforts that Mercury poured into the car. But as unsuccessful as the Cougar Eliminator was sales-wise, it nonetheless stands as one of the ultimate—and rarest—Mercury musclecars.

Chapter Three
Mopar Muscle

When you've got the King of Stock Car Racing, Richard Petty, in your camp, it's hard to fathom how you could be viewed as anything but serious about performance. And for Chrysler's Plymouth division, Petty was merely the icing on a multi-layer performance cake.

Beginning in the 1950s, Plymouth was making a reputation for itself as a performance car company, thanks to such models as the Fury and engines such as the original Hemi.

Along came the 1960s and drag racing literally took off. When it did, Plymouth was right there with its Super Stock 413 and 426 cars that cleaned the clocks of nearly anyone who bothered to run against them.

King Richard held court over NASCAR racing with his Petty Blue Plymouths (except for 1969 when he temporarily jumped ship to race a Torino Talladega for Ford). For 1970 Plymouth was right in the thick of

things with Petty at the wheel of its winged warrior, the Superbird.

Plymouths were regularly winning in one form of motorsports or another, and on the street. With such cars as the GTX, the Road Runner, and the legendary 'Cuda, Plymouth was able to earn its reputation every day of the week, often one stoplight at a time.

It's interesting to look back at each manufacturer's contributions to the musclecar era, to see what kind of mark each left. For Pontiac, it's clear that the GTO created the musclecar market. For Ford, it was the creation of the pony car market. Plymouth made the musclecar market fun. The Road Runner took its name from the popular cartoon character, and Plymouth played the connection for all it was worth by applying decals of the character to the car's exterior, interior, and even underhood. The company even gave the car a "beep-beep" horn. In 1970, when the end of the musclecar was on the horizon, Plymouth drenched its performance models in outlandish paint colors such as Panther Pink and Plum Crazy.

1964 Plymouth Sport Fury

Chrysler was no stranger to the drag strip. Nor did it find building a high-powered drag car any kind of mystery. So when drag racing competition started heating up in the early 1960s, it was no surprise to find Chrysler continually leading the pack with its "Max Wedge" engines.

By 1964, with the competition breathing down its neck with 409 Impalas, "swiss-cheesed" Super Duty Pontiacs, and quick-as-lightning Thunderbolts, Chrysler instructed its engineers to find more speed for the company's Super Stock offerings.

Starting with the simple logic that bigger is better, the engineers hogged out the aging 413 engine and came up with an additional 13 cubic inches of displacement. A new, short-runner, cross-ram-style intake manifold improved the engine's ability to breathe, while dual Carter four-barrels mixed fuel and air in ample volume. Two compression ratios were available with different power outputs—the "low" compression version used an 11.0:1 ratio that developed 415 horsepower, while the high-compression 13.5:1 engine made 10 additional horses. Regardless of compression, Chrysler gave the Super Stock engines an exotic exhaust system that consisted of unique, free-flowing,

Plymouth's 1964 Sport Fury was purpose-built to wage war on drag strips, and it soon proved a

individual runner cast-iron exhaust manifolds, 3-inch head pipes with a cross-over and dump tubes, and low-restriction twin mufflers for keeping things reasonably quiet on the street.

formidable opponent on the street thanks largely to its Super Stock 426. The Wedge-head 426 with a single four-barrel carb and 10.3:1 compression ratio developed 365 horsepower at 4,800 rpms.

Behind the Super Stock 426 engine, buyers could select either a heavy-duty four-speed manual gearbox or Chrysler's fortified 727 TorqueFlite, which was generally considered to be the preferable equipment due to the highly consistent times it allowed, plus its cushioning effect, which extended the life of such driveline parts as universal joints, axle gears, and axles.

The Super Stock 426 big-block was not an engine for the timid: the "weak" S/S 426 put out 415 horsepower; the hot 426 put out 10 more horsepower. Note the dual-quad cross-ram intake and exotic exhaust manifolds.

The 1964 Sport Fury's interior was quite comfortable with bucket seats. Deluxe appointments included a console, a large-diameter steering wheel, and even a four-instrument gauge panel.

With huge power and a seriously upgraded suspension system, the Super Stock Sport Fury was capable of catapult-like launches with a high-G pull that just didn't quit until the driver lost his nerve or the road ended—either of which happened in a hurry. On the strip, stock S/S Sport Furys could run low-14s out of the box with inexperienced drivers at the wheel. Experienced drivers could rip off 13s until the cows came home. And with some tweaking and a few carefully selected aftermarket parts, including headers and slicks, mostly stock S/S Sport Furys were honest-to-goodness 12-second cars.

Apart from their bulletproof powertrains, the Sport Fury and its sibling, the Polara-based Super Stock Dodge, had a weight advantage compared to their usual competition. At 3,400 pounds, the Chrysler twins were the lightest cars in their class. When GM and Ford tried to even the scales by swapping in lightweight hoods, fenders, and bumpers, Chrysler responded in kind, dropping the Fury's weight to just over the 3,200-pound NHRA class minimum.

But the Plymouths (and Dodges) would likely have continued their winning ways without any exotic

weight-loss programs. The cars were simply that good on the strip.

In the showroom, the Fury proved to be one of Plymouth's most attractive models ever—a characteristic many Mopar enthusiasts still respect about the model. But even the non-Mopar-minded admit the Super Stock Sport Fury was an awesome performer.

The Fabulous Chrysler B-Bodies

In 1966, Chrysler's mid-size cars were not as flashy as their contemporaries from General Motors and Ford. General Motors' and Ford's musclecars were given special trim and badges announcing their high-performance heritage to the world. On the street, it was easy to spot a Pontiac GTO, a Chevy 396SS, or a Ford Fairlane GT. Chrysler took a much more low-key approach to its musclecars, especially the Hemi. All 1966 B-bodies, from both Dodge and Plymouth, were built on the previous year's platforms. It would have been difficult at night on Woodward Avenue to read the small HEMI badging on the side of a 1966 Belvedere or Coronet. But as soon as the light turned green, the Hemi would be gone like a shot.

For 1966 the entire Dodge line was restyled. The Coronet 500 was the top-of-the-line model, but compared to its 1966 musclecar contemporaries, it lacked panache.

The 1966 Dodge Coronet

The Dodge Coronet was offered in four trim levels: the base Coronet, the Coronet Deluxe, and the Coronet 440 and 500. The 440 and 500 were only used to distinguish the differences in the series of cars and had nothing to do with engine size. The 1966 Coronet featured a finely sculpted body in both sedan and hardtop versions. Car buyers were accustomed to seeing something new each year, and the new Coronet didn't disappoint its fans. The big news was the addition of the powerful 426-ci street Hemi engine to the option list. Dodge now had a full-fledged musclecar. Unfortunately, the new Coronet didn't have the visual appeal to match its horsepower, but that would soon change. Hemi sales were brisk, with over 740 Coronet customers checking the box on the order sheet for the elephant engine.

In 1966, the Hemi engine came in a wide variety of models, including this Coronet Deluxe two-door sedan. Looking more like grandma's grocery-getter, this sedan surprised more than a few people on the street.

The 1966 Plymouth Belvedere/Satellite models, like the Dodges, were restyled. The availability of the Hemi engine in showroom models, like this Belvedere convertible, allowed NASCAR competitors like Richard Petty to race Hemi-powered cars on the track.

The 1966 Plymouth Belvedere and Satellite

Like the Dodge Coronet, the 1966 Plymouth Belvedere and Satellite both had gracefully contoured sides. At 116 inches, the Plymouth rode on a wheelbase one inch shorter than the Coronet.

The 426 Hemi engine installed in the 1966 Coronets and Belvederes was a detuned version of the race Hemi that had a lowered compression ratio of 10.25:1 and a milder cam. The only transmissions available were a four-speed manual and a heavy-duty TorqueFlite.

Announcing the Hemi 426 Plymouth Belvedere

Now what this country needs is a dragstrip with a couple of good hairpin curves.

The Hemi-powered Plymouth Belvedere: a high-performance 426-cubic-inch hemispherical-head V-8. Dual four-barrel carbs. Dual-breaker distributor. High-lift, high-overlap cam. Special plugs, pistons and double valve springs. Low back pressure dual exhaust system. Blue Streak Special tires. Wide-rim wheels. Oversize front torsion bars. Sway bar. Added-leaf, high-rate rear springs. Firm-Ride shocks.

And every Belvedere Satellite has: Front bucket seats. Center console with glove box. Deep-pile carpeting. Padded instrument panel. Safety-Rim wheels. 3-speed automatic or 4-on-the-floor stick, optional. Like an iron fist in a velvet glove, the Hemi 426 Plymouth Belvedere.

PLYMOUTH DIVISION ★ CHRYSLER MOTORS CORPORATION

Plymouth ...a great car by Chrysler Corporation.

In 1966, the marketing staff at Plymouth didn't waste any time advertising the new Hemi engine's availability or its performance potential. Plymouth placed ads like this one touting the new Belvedere in enthusiast magazines.

The April 1966 issue of *Car and Driver* featured a road test of a new Hemi-powered Plymouth Satellite. In the article's opening paragraph, the writer makes reference to the previous month's edition, in which the magazine compared six of the hottest new "Super Cars." Unfortunately, the Hemi wasn't delivered in time for that issue's test. If it had been, it would have resoundingly trounced every car there. "Without cheating, without expensive NASCAR mechanics, without towing or trailing the Plymouth to the test-track," the writer said, "it went faster, rode better,

stopped better, and caused fewer problems than all six of the cars tested last month." It was interesting to note that prior to the test, the Hemi Satellite had been driven by magazine staffers from Detroit to New York and then used as a daily driver for a week. The only complaints about the new Plymouth were the location of the tachometer (on the console) and the less-than-impressive styling. The demand was high for Plymouth's new Hemi power, and more than 1,500 were sold in Belvedere I, Belvedere II, and Satellite models in 1966.

The 1967 Plymouth GTX was the first Hemi car whose appearance equaled its performance. Nonfunctional hood scoops were standard on the GTX, but the sport stripes were optional.

The 1967 Plymouth GTX

The Plymouth Belvedere and Dodge Coronet returned in 1967 with only a few changes to the grille and taillights, but the new top-of-the-line models, the Plymouth GTX and the Dodge R/T, made their debuts. The GTX was Plymouth's first shot at musclecar styling, and it was dead center on target. Available only in a two-door hardtop or convertible, the 1967 GTX featured twin nonfunctional hood scoops. A quick-fill racing style gas cap was prominent on the left quarter panel. Dual sport stripes and chrome road wheels were optional. When they were added, the GTX had the sporty styling musclecar buyers were looking for. The 440-ci V-8 producing 375 horsepower was standard. The 426 Hemi was optional, but it came with a heavy-duty suspension. The GTX's interior featured saddle-grain vinyl with an attractive tooled leather insert on the seats. Front bucket seats with a center console were standard, and the rear seats were styled to look like bucket seats. The GTX sold well and 125 Hemis made up a fraction of the total of 12,690 units that reached dealers. In the 1967

Plymouth line of Belvederes, Satellites, and GTXs, there were just slightly fewer than 200 equipped with the Hemi engine.

The GTX was fitted with the 375-horsepower Super Commando 440 V-8.

The 1967 Plymouth GTX had clean sculpted sides that made an exciting styling package. The racing style gas cap on the left quarter panel was also part of the GTX package.

Chrome road wheels were an option on the 1967 GTX, but redline tires were standard. In addition to the Hemi badges on the front fender, there was a small one on the rear edge of the deck lid.

The 1967 GTX's stylish interior had front buckets and a chrome center console in which the tachometer was mounted. The "Inland" shifter, named for its manufacturer, selected the gears for the four-speed transmission. It wasn't until 1968 that Hurst shifters became standard equipment.

Standard GTX performance was provided by the 375-horsepower Super Commando 440, but the 425-horsepower 426 street Hemi was also available. At 3,545 pounds and 200.5 inches long, the GTX fit into the full-size musclecar category; but equipped with the killer 426 Hemi, it humbled most of its opponents.

The 1967 GTX was available in either a hardtop or a convertible. Although the 1967 models used the same sheet metal as the 1966, the grille was modified to accept quad headlights. *Dale Amy*

The 1967 GTX was touted as Plymouth's "Supercar." The standard engine was a 440 with a TorqueFlite, and the only optional engine was the Hemi. Even though Plymouth had finally put together a true musclecar package, the Hemi GTXs, because of the added cost, didn't sell well. This GTX convertible is one of 17 built. *Dale Amy*

In 1967 Dodge introduced its new performance model, the R/T (Road and Track). Like the GTX, it came standard with a 440 engine and a host of heavy-duty performance-oriented features. And like the GTX,

The 1967 Dodge R/T

Dodge introduced its own version of the musclecar, the R/T (Road and Track). The R/T was a Dodge version of the Plymouth GTX. It featured a grille that was similar in styling to that of the Charger's, but the Dodge R/T's headlights were exposed. Three large nonfunctional louvers adorned the center of the hood. Available in only two-door hardtop and convertible body styles, the R/T rode on a heavy-duty suspension. Bucket seats were standard and chrome road wheels were optional. The R/T also featured the 375-horsepower 440 as standard equipment. In 1967, street Hemi engines were installed

the only optional engine was the 425-horsepower 426 Hemi.

in 283 Dodge R/Ts, and 117 Hemi engines were installed in the balance of the 1967 Coronet line. While the 1967 Plymouth GTX and Dodge Coronet R/T were outstanding musclecars, complete performance and styling packages (à la GTO and SS396) for the B-body Dodge and Plymouth B-bodies would have to wait until 1968.

The 1967 R/T featured the same grille as the Charger but without the hidden headlights. On top of the hood were three large simulated louvers. This Hemi-powered R/T convertible was one of only two built in 1967.

Plymouth's introduction of the Road Runner in 1968 was big news. The finely trimmed GTX was still available, and it featured the same hood as the Road Runner with side-facing nonfunctional scoops. The GTX also had twin body side stripes that terminated at the GTX emblem on the quarter panel. *Mopar Muscle*

The Plymouth Road Runner

In 1968, with one giant leap, Chrysler made a major advancement in the musclecar wars with the release of the new Road Runner. It was the shot in the arm Plymouth needed. The 1967 GTX with all the muscle-car options cost considerably more and never had the streetwise look of the GTO. Plymouth decided to strip

its newly restyled mid-size entry of any frills, then add a performance engine package and a whimsical cartoon name. With the Road Runner, Plymouth had a low-priced factory hot rod that was capable of kicking any GTO's butt at any stoplight.

The 1968 Plymouth line included the base Belvedere, Road Runner, and GTX. They were all restyled in a

smoother, more integrated look. The wheelbase remained at 116 inches, but the track width, front and rear, increased by one-half inch. The GTX also came with bucket seats, a center console, and lots of imitation woodgrain trim. The exterior featured extra chrome trim along the rocker panel and around the wheel openings. A few inches above the rocker panel were two horizontal body stripes that terminated with a large GTX chrome emblem just in front of the rear wheel opening. The GTX's hood featured twin side-facing vents within which the engine size was inset in small chrome letters. Drive-in restaurant regulars and musclecar enthusiasts knew that the 1967 GTX came with a standard 440-ci engine, as did the 1968 model. Once again, the Hemi engine was an option and 446 was so equipped.

As nice as the GTX was, the Road Runner got all the press in 1968. Its beauty was in its simplicity. Stripped of all extra chrome, it looked as docile as a librarian's sedan. The Road Runner was initially introduced as a two-door coupe. The hardtop would be introduced later in the model year, but no convertible Road Runner models were offered in 1968. The grille was the same egg-crate design as the Belvedere, but it was accented in black. The Road Runner used the same hood—with side-facing nonfunctional vents—as the GTX. A small chrome plate near the front edge of the doors discreetly announced that this was a Road Runner. To the rear of this Road Runner emblem was a small decal of the crafty little bird at warp speed. A standing version of the bird was placed on the Road Runner's deck lid. As the year progressed, a Decor Group was added to the Road Runner, which included

In 1968, many options were added to the Road Runner, including bucket seats. An 8000-rpm tachometer was integrated into the right side of the instrument cluster. If someone forgot what model of car they were riding in, all they had to do was look at the right side of the instrument panel to see the smirking face of the little bird.

a deck lid decal featuring the bird at full speed, trailed by a cloud of dust.

The Road Runner's bench seat interior was initially offered in blue, parchment, or black and silver. When Plymouth introduced the Decor Group, it added gold, red, green, black, and white to the interior color list. Bucket seats were not a Road Runner option in 1968.

The standard engine for the Road Runner was a special version of the 383, producing 335 horsepower and 425 foot-pounds of torque. A four-speed transmission was standard, and a column-shifted TorqueFlite was optional. There was only one optional engine for the 1968 Road Runner—the Hemi. Like the 383, the Hemi came standard with a four-speed, but the TorqueFlite was a no-cost option. The Performance Axle Package, which included the Dana Sure-Grip rear axle, was a required option. Along with the Hemi engine option came a larger radiator, power front disc brakes, and 15-inch wheels with F-70 Polyglas tires. In 1968, a total of 1,011 customers paid the extra $714 for the Hemi option; of these, 840 bought coupes and 171 bought hardtops.

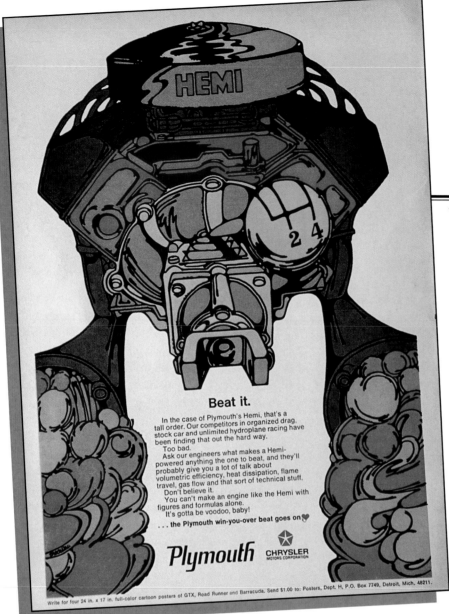

The artwork of Peter Max was fashionable in the late 1960s. Plymouth took advantage of it in this slick *Hot Rod* magazine advertisement to promote the Hemi engine.

In the early and mid-1960s, Charlie Di Bari was the spark plug who provided the fire to the successful Melrose Missile race car program. The Di Bari family owned Melrose Motors and soon became the northern California Mopar high-performance Mecca. "Shortly after the Road Runners came out," recalls Di Bari, "we wanted to do something that would create a stir, calling more attention to the car and to the dealership. At that time, if you had a minimum of five cars, you could have any car painted a special color. We had five Road Runners painted Omaha Orange.

They came in and went right out! We didn't want to have all orange cars, so then we had some painted school bus yellow and then a bright green color. Those were the first three, and the most dominant, of the special colors we came up with." The brightly colored Road Runners were an immediate hit, and soon customers were clamoring for them. Plymouth's marketing personnel in Detroit saw how fast the market was scooping them up. Vivid colors were formerly reserved for trucks but were now part of Chrysler's new musclecar palette.

HEMI ROAD RUNNER: 0-105 IN 13.5 SECS.! ONE OF THE REASONS MOTOR TREND NAMED IT...

CAR OF THE YEAR

See facts, figures, NHRA acceleration times — Page 127.

In 1969, the Road Runner was named *Motor Trend* magazine's Car of the Year. Never missing a chance to stomp the competition on the street, track, or in print ads, the marketing staff at Plymouth proudly heralded the announcement. The text of the ad went on to describe the quarter-mile times a stock Hemi Road Runner clocked, and the few simple modifications required to improve those times.

In 1968 the mid-size muscle market was filled with a host of competitors. Fresh designs and a long list of performance options were what it took to stay in the game. Dodge reskinned its Coronet with slippery sheet metal that featured sculpted quarter panels. The successful R/T option returned in both hardtop and convertible models. With the R/T, the customer had the choice of side stripes or Bumblebee stripes. The standard engine for the R/T was the 440-ci engine. In 1968, 220 Dodge R/Ts were sold with the Hemi engine.

The 1968 Dodge Super Bee

The big news for Dodge in 1968 was the release of the Super Bee option, which hit the Dodge showrooms in February 1968. It was designed to be a low-priced performance car in the same mold as the 1968 Road Runner. Based on the 440 coupe, the Super Bee featured swing-out quarter windows and had the same power-bulge hood as the R/T. Bumblebee stripes and a circular Super Bee logo on the quarter panel appeared on the rear of the car. The Super Bee's standard engine and transmission was a 335-horsepower 383, backed by

The 1969 Road Runner continued the momentum of the 1968 model. In the Road Runner, the public was offered a highly identifiable musclecar at a low price. In addition, engine options and creature comforts were available at an extra cost.

a four-speed. The Hemi was optional and 125 were delivered in 1968.

The 1969 Road Runner

In 1969, the Road Runner returned with a vengeance. Plymouth sold 80,000, almost double the previous year's total. Only minor changes were made to the 1969 model's grille and taillights. The Road Runner was still the low-priced performance king, but the price was increasing and the option list was expanding. A convertible Road Runner joined the coupe and hardtop models. Power windows, center console, and bucket seats were new to the option list. Standard on any Hemi and optional for the 383, was a Fresh Air hood. This hood was also used on the GTX. It was similar to the hood on the 1968 Road Runner, except the vents were vertical. Extending under the hood was a system of ductwork that directed

fresh air to the engine. Added to the 1969 Road Runner engine option list was the three two-barrel carburetor-equipped 440. Dubbed the 440 Six-Barrel, it came with a nasty-looking black scooped hood and many of the Hemi's heavy-duty suspension components. This powerful engine offered Hemi-style acceleration at half the cost.

Motor Trend magazine selected the 1969 Road Runner as the Car of the Year. In multi-page ads celebrating the fact, Plymouth copywriters went on to give the specific numbers the potential buyers wanted to hear—quarter-mile times and speeds. In stock form, a 1969 Hemi Road Runner, equipped with a TorqueFlite and 4.10 rear axle, consistently ran the quarter-mile in the mid-13-second range at speeds of 105 miles per hour. The next day, the same car was brought back to the track with a few bolt-on performance additions. A Racer Brown cam and kit were added along with a set

The 1969 Road Runner was available in three body styles: a two-door coupe, a hardtop (shown), and a convertible. The cartoon character adorned each door and the center of the deck lid. Also on the left side of the deck lid was a small Hemi emblem. The 15-inch wheels were standard with the Hemi option.

of Hooker headers. Run with the headers open, the Hemi Road Runner's elapsed times dropped by seven-tenths of a second and speeds improved by five miles per hour.

While overall sales of the 1969 Road Runner increased, the number of buyers opting for the Hemi decreased slightly. The hardtops led the list with 422 Hemis, followed by the coupes at 356, and the convertibles at a lowly 10.

Like the Road Runner, the 1969 GTX saw only minor changes. The grille was redesigned and a GTX emblem was added to the center. In the rear, the taillights were recessed. The body side stripes and chrome molding were removed from the rocker panel and replaced with a flat black lower-body treatment. The GTX shared the Road Runner's Fresh Air hood on its standard 440 and optional Hemi. The success of the

Road Runner took a bite out of GTX sales, with only 15,608 units delivered in 1969, which was down 3,300 units compared to 1968 sales. Hemi sales were down accordingly, with only 198 hardtops and 11 convertibles delivered.

The 1969 Dodge performance lineup made very few changes to the R/T and Super Bee from their 1968 models. Bumblebee stripes on both models were revised to a single broad stripe. Both the R/T and Super Bee were available with an optional pair of dummy side scoops, which were attached to the leading edge of the quarter panel. The Super Bee, only available as a two-door coupe previously, was now available in a hardtop, and bucket seats were an option. The most significant change for both models was the addition of the Ram Charger hood. Standard with the Hemi and optional with other performance

In 1970, both the Plymouth and Dodge were restyled. The Dodge's dual loop grille received mixed reviews, and Plymouth R/Ts featured nonfunctional quarter panel scoops and twin hood scoops that were functional. When the model was equipped with a 426 engine, a small HEMI emblem was placed on each hood scoop.

engines, the Ram Charger hood fed fresh air to the carburetors. On the surface of the hood were attached two forward-facing wedge-shaped scoops. Under the hood was a large fiberglass fixture that fed fresh air to the air cleaner. Models with the optional Hemi engine had HEMI spelled out in small chrome letters on the outboard side of each scoop. In 1969, a total of 258 Super Bees and 107 Coronet R/Ts were equipped with the Hemi engine.

The 1970 Coronet

In 1970 the Dodge Coronet was restyled with a unique front-end treatment. The grille had a wide split in the center, and each side was fitted with a halo-style bumper that tapered as it reached toward that split. It had the look of someone with large nostrils scowling. This would be the final year for the Coronet R/T and Super Bee. In 1971 both of these models would be listed as Charger options.

The 1970 R/T and Super Bee

But in 1970, R/T and Super Bee meant performance. The R/T was available in both hardtop and convertible body styles, whereas the Super Bee was available only in a two-door coupe or hardtop. The R/T side scoop was redesigned with a single forward-facing opening. Bumblebee stripes were again part of the R/T and Super Bee option and could be deleted. With the 1970 Super Bee, the customer could opt for an alternate set of stripes, known as the "reverse C-stripes." They were two hockey stick–style stripes that traced the quarter panel character lines. A larger circular Super Bee decal was placed at the point where they met on the rear of the quarter panel. With the Hemi option, on both the R/T and Super Bee, the Ram Charger hood was standard. The musclecar insurance crackdown was in full swing in 1970, and performance cars including the R/T and Super Bee suffered. Sales in 1970 for the Super Bee were 15,506 units and 2,615 for the R/T. A mere 38 1970 Super Bees were sold with the Hemi option. Hemi-equipped 1970 R/Ts are even more rare, with just 14 sold, and only 1 of those was a convertible. These would be the last Coronet-based cars available with the Hemi engine, and the only mid-size Dodge Hemis sold in 1971 would be Charger Super Bee and Charger R/T models.

The 1970 Road Runner and GTX

The 1970 Road Runner and GTX models were also restyled and were a little more mainstream compared to the 1970 Dodge Coronet. Plymouth's designers were able to use the roof and doors from the 1969 model and add new quarter panels, taillight treatment, and new front-end sheet metal for a fresh look. The quarter panels featured more-rounded corners and had a small nonfunctional scoop on the leading edge. The twin vertical vents were removed from the hood, and a power dome was added. The new Air Grabber

The 1970 Dodge R/T's interior was well appointed. A woodgrain and chrome console divided the two standard high-back bucket seats covered in Shallow Elk grain vinyl. The instrument panel also featured woodgrain appliqués. The two large dials on the left side of the instrument cluster are the speedometer and tachometer/clock combination.

scoop was standard on the Hemi-equipped GTXs and Road Runners. The driver could flip a switch under the instrument panel that would open the trap door Air Grabber scoop. Wonderfully creative graphics on the side of the scoop would then be visible as outside air was directed to the engine. This scoop won big style points on the street.

The 15-inch wheels, which had been a standard part of the GTX and Road Runner Hemi package, were no longer required, and all Hemis came standard with 14x6-inch wheels, with the 15-inch wheels becoming an option. The Road Runner was available in a two-door coupe, hardtop, or convertible. The GTX, available only as a hardtop, had a twin body stripe that started at the leading edge of the front fender and swept rearward into the quarter panel scoop. Like their brothers over in the Dodge camp, the Plymouth executives were able to read the writing on the wall—musclecar mania was winding down. In 1970, only 152 buyers specified a Hemi engine in the Road Runner, and GTX customers were just as reluctant, buying only 72 Hemis.

The completely restyled 1971 Road Runner had the rounded look of the new body that made the car look larger than it actually was. When a Hemi was ordered, an Air Grabber hood scoop was included in the center of the domed hood.

The 1971 Road Runner and GTX

In 1971, the only Hemi B-body was the Plymouth Road Runner and GTX. The Belvedere name was dropped and all two-door models were hardtops that were now called Satellite Sebrings. Plymouth offered no convertible in 1971. Both the 1971 Road Runner and GTX were based on this fully redesigned Satellite Sebring. The new Plymouth offerings and the Dodge Chargers now shared the same 115-inch platform, although the Plymouth body was 2.2 inches shorter. The new body appeared larger and more rounded than the 1970 model. The front end had a long, low hood line that extended out to a flush fitting halo-style bumper. The grille and headlights were sunk deeply into the

The Hemi engine was indicated by decals above the side marker light. *Dale Amy*

Aggressive front and rear wheel–opening flares high-lighted the clean styling of the 1971 Road Runner. Road Runner graphics were placed on the quarter panel just above the wheel opening and enclosed in a circle on the right side of the deck lid. Only 55 Road Runners were equipped with the Hemi engine in 1971, the last year of production. *Dale Amy*

bumper. The full wheel openings were flared out slightly. This feature, along with a wider track, gave the new Road Runner and GTX a very aggressive look. Both the GTX and Road Runner offered body-colored bumpers as an option, and a transverse strobe stripe was optional for the Road Runner. It ran from the rear wheel opening forward across the C-pillar and roof and then back down the C-pillar to the other rear wheel opening. With the Hemi engine, the Air Grabber hood was again standard.

In 1971, the curtain officially came down on the musclecar era. A total of 55 Hemi-powered Road Runners and 35 Hemi-powered GTXs were sold that year. Emission constraints and auto insurance surcharges had finally sucked the oxygen out of the musclecar atmosphere.

The Winged Wonders and Chargers

Chrysler's management was unhappy with the public's poor response to the 1962 Plymouths and Dodges. Sales for that year were dismal compared to the rest of the industry. Chrysler's management wanted its cars to have a cleaner, more mainstream design. Elwood Engle, a Ford designer, was hired to replace Virgil Exner, Chrysler's premier designer during the 1950s. Engle was given the formidable task of reshaping Chrysler's look and doing it in minimal time. To make Engle's task more monumental, two new cars were added, the Plymouth Barracuda and the Dodge Charger.

The Dodge Charger was conceived as an upscale personal luxury car in the same mode as the Buick Riviera, Olds Toronado, and Ford Thunderbird, but less costly. The new Charger was to lead the Dodge Rebellion advertising theme in presenting a new image of performance and clean, inventive design.

The 1966 Dodge Charger

The 1966 Charger shared its platform with the 117-inch wheelbase Coronet. Both cars shared the front- and side-sheet metal, but the Charger's fastback roofline dramatically set it apart. Because of the Charger's hardtop design, a considerable amount of body structure had to be added in the areas of the C-pillars and the upper rear deck. Dodge designers made small but significant changes to the Coronet's quarter panels. The rear wheel openings were enlarged and shaped the same as the front wheel openings, which gave the Charger an aggressive, sporty stance. The leading edge of the quarter panels received two horizontal depressions that simulated air intakes. The sides of the Charger were clean and devoid of any trim other than a thin belt line molding, a rocker panel molding, and thin wheel lip moldings. The large triangular sail panel was accented with a tasteful CHARGER name plate.

The Charger's front-end treatment was also bold. Within the large rectangular opening was a full-width grille with hidden headlights. The grille consisted of a series of thin vertical chrome bars, whose density concealed the split lines for the headlight doors and the parking lights. Even when the headlight doors were open, the lights were fully trimmed. It was a small detail that few manufacturers took time to master with hidden headlights. One plague that afflicts cars with

Heading the Dodge Rebellion advertising program in 1966 was the smartly styled Charger. It was built on the Coronet platform, and Chrysler designers

hidden headlights are doors that fail to open or close completely. This "lazy eye" look neutralizes the overall effect of hidden headlights and makes noncustomers out of potential customers. Chrysler engineers were given the job of designing a failproof mechanism. To accomplish this, they gave each light its own heavily geared electric motor. When the driver pulled the light switch, a red light illuminated on the instrument panel until the headlight doors were fully open. An override switch was provided to open the doors in icy weather or to clean the headlight lenses.

The rear of the Charger carried the same wide rectangular one-piece look as the front. Within a thin chrome molding was a large single taillight lens. Widely spaced

A full-length console, mounting an optional clock, split both the 1966 Charger's front and rear bucket seats. The chrome instrument panel's two center pods contained the 150-mile-per-hour speedometer and the 6,000-rpm tachometer.

incorporated a full-width grille that cleverly disguised its hidden headlights and parking lights in amongst the vertical bars.

individual chrome letters spelled out CHARGER across the width of the lens. The 1966 Charger looked long, low, and wide. In addition, the execution of the exterior sheet metal and details was crisp and contemporary.

The Charger's interior was as fashionable as its exterior. It featured individual seating for four. The front seats were Chryslers new clamshell-design buckets. The rear seats were also buckets, with backrests that could fold down, converting the small luggage compartment into one of extended length. Splitting the seats was a full-length console, trimmed with a die-cast chrome plate with a brushed aluminum appliqué. At the forward end, a clock was mounted in a chrome housing. In keeping with the sporty theme, all 1966 Dodge

Chargers with optional engines came with a floor-mounted shifter for either the TorqueFlite automatic or four-speed manual transmission. The instrument panel held four large chrome-rimmed pods. The two pods in the center housed the speedometer and a 6,000 rpm tachometer.

Dodge defined the Charger's performance image with the selection of standard and optional engines. The 318-ci 230-horsepower V8 was the base engine, and the 361- and 383-ci engines and the 426-ci street Hemi were optional. Along with the Hemi engine came a heavy-duty suspension, which featured 11-inch brake drums.

Even though it was introduced late in the model year, the 1966 Dodge Charger sold well. Of the 37,344 that were produced, 468 were equipped with the Hemi engine. Drag racers didn't latch onto the Charger like the NASCAR crowd did. The sleek aerodynamics and extra weight were counterproductive to the drag-racing credo. But down South, the good ol' boys of NASCAR saw the advantages of the slick roofline and powerful

Hemi engine. David Pearson, driving a Dodge Charger, won the NASCAR Grand National championship.

Chrysler didn't want to alter a successful car, and it made only minor changes to the 1967 Charger. The 440-ci engine was added to the option list. But in 1967, sales of the Charger were dismal—less than half those of the previous year. Sales of the Hemi engine dropped even more dramatically, down to 118.

Four V-8 engines were available in the 1966 Charger, including the 426 Hemi. In 1966, all Hemi engines came with a large chrome-plated air cleaner and black crinkle-painted valve covers. Adjusting the valve lash was a lengthy project because items like heater hoses had to be removed in order to take off the large valve cover.

The 1966 Charger's full-width taillight matched the design theme of the front end, and the rear window's outer edges curled up to meet the sweeping roofline.

For the second-generation Dodge Charger, Chrysler designers were determined to create a car that looked completely different from the Coronet. Their vision was a car that looked as though it could be driven directly from the street to the high banks of Daytona. The new Charger featured a wedge-shape body, fastback roofline, and aggressive bulges around each full wheel opening. *Dale Amy*

The Second Generation Charger

For the 1968 model year, Chrysler designer Bill Brownlie was determined to create a Charger that looked completely different from the Coronet. His vision was a car that could be driven directly to the high banks of Daytona but could also be toured on the street. Design staff members got busy and submitted their renderings to Brownlie. The designer who shared Brownlie's vision was Richard Tighstin, and his sketches showed a car with a narrow front end that got wider toward the rear. Tighstin's side profile showed the car's wedge shape with a built-in rear spoiler. This would be the second-generation Charger.

The new Charger carried many of the same styling cues as the original, including the full-width rectangular grille and large front and rear wheel openings. The body on the new Charger lost its angular lines in favor of a smooth, Coke-bottle shape. The sheet metal at each wheel opening was raised and flared slightly. The black-out grille carried hidden headlights and thin vertical bars similar to the first-generation Charger's grille. The subtle quarter panel scoops on the earlier Charger were moved up to the doors, and an additional set was cut into the hood. Within the scalloped hood scoops was an optional set of turn indicators. Keeping in sync with the racing theme, Chrysler designers added a large quick-fill gas cap on top of the left quarter panel. The Charger's flat rear window tunneled into the fastback roofline. In the rear, the full-width taillight of the 1966 and 1967 models was dropped in favor of two pairs of circular lights set into an angled panel. The interior of the new Charger was not as well detailed as the previous model had been. The seats, buckets in front and bench rear, were less supportive, but still attractive. The instrument panel had the efficiency of an aircraft cockpit, with two large dials on the left (clock and 150-mile-per-hour speedometer) and four smaller gauges on the right. An optional tachometer was integrated into the clock.

The Charger R/T

The chassis and engine combinations for the 1968 Charger were carryovers from 1967. In 1968, a new model was added to the Charger—the R/T (Road and Track). The R/T was a performance package that offered a standard 375-horsepower 440-ci engine and a host of heavy-duty components. TorqueFlite was the standard transmission, and a four-speed manual was optional. Also standard were rear Bumblebee stripes, but the graphics could be deleted. The Hemi engine was only available with the R/T package, and in 1968 475 were sold.

The 1969 Charger was released with very few changes from the 1968 model, but the most notable change was the addition of a center split in the grille. In the rear, a new pair of rectangular-shaped taillights, reminiscent of those on the 1967 Charger, replaced the circular ones. The Hemi engine was again available only with the R/T option, and 432 were delivered in 1969.

The Charger 500

Certain aspects of the new Charger's exterior, while stylish, hindered performance. The deep-set grille and tunneled rear window were detrimental to high speed. Late in the 1968 model year, Chrysler designed a modified version it named the Charger 500, which would be released as a 1969 model. The Charger 500 featured a flush-mounted grille and a rear window that followed the sloping shape of the C-pillars. This flush-mounted rear window required a special shortened deck lid. A Bumblebee stripe ran across the back, with the number 500 on the quarter panel. NASCAR required that a minimum of 500 production-line cars be built in order to qualify for competition. The intent of the rule was to eliminate the building of special race-only cars that weren't available to the general public.

The Charger 500s were equipped with a standard 440 engine at a base price of $3,591 or the optional Hemi at an additional $648.20. A TorqueFlite or a four-speed manual were the only two transmissions available. Records show that only 67 Charger 500s were Hemi powered. *Hot Rod* magazine had three of these Hemi-powered Charger 500s available for road tests for its February 1969 issue. Unfortunately, one of the two four-speed cars was stolen just prior to the test. Of the two Hemi 500s, staffer Steve Kelly favored the TorqueFlite-equipped 500. He wrote, "This is the kind of car you make excuses to drive." One option he heartily recommended was front disc brakes. Both Charger 500s were run at the drags. The four-speed car was equipped with a 4.10 rear axle and ran the best times at 13.48 seconds and a speed of 109 miles per hour. The TorqueFlite was mated to a 3.23 rear axle on the other Hemi Charger 500, and it ran the quarter in 13.8 seconds at a speed of 105 miles per hour.

The Charger 500, with its revised aerodynamics, faced the Torino Talladega and Mercury Cyclone Spoiler with their modified front ends in NASCAR competition. Whatever the Charger 500 had gained in aerodynamics was now equaled by the Fords and Mercurys. To gain the competitive edge, Chrysler pulled out all the stops with the Charger Daytona.

The modifications made to the 1969 Dodge Charger 500 were designed for NASCAR competition. The grille was pulled forward, flush to the edge of the opening. The hidden headlights were dropped in favor of exposed quad units, and the A-pillars received a special piece of bright trim.

In the rear, the Daytona 500's rear window was blended flush with the C-pillars, creating a smooth flow of air over the roof. The rear window placement and subsequent roof modifications required a severe shortening of the deck lid. The taillight treatment and quick release-style gas cap were standard on all Chargers, but the transverse Bumblebee stripes were only on the Charger 500.

The 1969 Charger Daytona

The 1969 Charger Daytona was the most outrageous and infamous of all the Dodge Chargers. It was Chrysler's throw-down-the-gauntlet approach to building an unbeatable car for NASCAR competition. Costs to Chrysler for the Daytona were rumored to be as high as $1 million. The Charger Daytona picked up where the Charger 500 left off. It retained the 500's flush-mounted rear window, but used a new nose piece and rear wing developed in a wind tunnel. The wedge-shaped nose was constructed of sheet metal and added 18 inches to the front of the car. Rear-facing scoops were added to the tops of the front fenders for tire clearance on the race versions. Engineers added a rear spoiler that was 58 inches wide. It was supported by 23.5-inch-high uprights that grew out of the top of the quarter panels. This wing was adjustable, and it canceled the lift created at the rear of the car. The rear of the Charger Daytona was adorned with a wide Bumblebee stripe that covered the wing. Emblazoned in large letters on the quarter panel was the name DAYTONA. These body modifications reduced the aerodynamic drag by 15 percent over the Charger 500, thus greatly enhancing the Charger Daytona's top speed. Chrysler's adventures into the heady world of aerodynamics paid off with a car that could easily reach and maintain speeds of 200 miles per hour. It was also a public relations success. Other than the race cars, only 503 Charger Daytonas were built in 1969, and only 70 of those had the Hemi engine.

The Charger Daytona proved to be an excellent performer on the high banks. When it made its first appearance at NASCAR's Talladega race in September 1969, it quickly became the fastest stock car in history when Charlie Glotzbach took the pole for the Talladega 500 with a speed of 199.466 miles per hour. The anticipated showdown against the Fords didn't materialize. The Ford drivers withdrew, citing unsafe conditions, and Richard Brickhouse won the race in a Charger Daytona.

Legend has it that because of the success of the Charger Daytona, Richard Petty wanted to switch to a Dodge Charger Daytona, but he was under contract to drive a Plymouth. The people at Plymouth refused to let him compete in a Dodge, so Petty defected and drove a Ford for the 1969 season. In 1970, Petty would return behind the wheel of Plymouth's new winged car, the Superbird.

The 1970 Plymouth Superbird

The 1970 Plymouth Superbird had the assertive good looks of the 1969 Charger Daytona. Like its Dodge Daytona brother, the Superbird was built and sold to the general public to comply with NASCAR rules. At first glance it appears as if the Daytona parts were simply bolted onto a Road Runner to create the Superbird, but they weren't. All Superbird components were unique to that car. The extended nosecone, which housed hidden headlights, had a small rubber strip across the front. Just under the leading edge, there was an opening for air to enter the radiator. To fit the nosecone onto the Road Runner, the leading edges of the front fenders and the hood were extended to match the nosecone's surface. The rearward-facing scoops were placed over the front tires and were the same color as the body work. The Superbird's rear window was also unique. Along with roof and rear deck modifications, the rear window was designed to improve aerodynamics. To facilitate the speedy assembly of the street versions, all Superbirds sold to the general public were equipped

Even Wile E. Coyote on an Acme rocket sled would have a hard time catching this Lemon Twist-colored

with a vinyl top. This precluded expensive metal finishing that would have required extra time and expense. Rising from the top of the quarter panels were the uprights that supported the rear wing. The Superbird's uprights were much wider at the base than those on the Charger Daytona.

All Superbirds came standard with the 440-ci engine with either a single four-barrel carburetor or the six-

Superbird. Based on a 1970 Road Runner, it featured much of the same wind-cheating design tricks that were used on the Daytona 500. All Superbirds came with Rallye wheels.

barrel configuration of three two-barrel Holleys. The Hemi was also optional and 135 Superbirds were so equipped. All Superbirds came with an all vinyl interior in black, or white with black trim. A bench seat was standard and front bucket seats were optional. The instrumentation was the same as on the 1970 Road Runner. The exterior colors for the Superbird were limited to Alpine White, Petty Blue, Lemon Twist, TorRed, Burnt Orange Metallic, Vitamin C Orange, Limelight, or Blue Fire Metallic. The Superbird's racing culture was distinctively shown by its graphics. On the quarter panel was a large decal that spelled out the word PLYMOUTH in the same size and font as Richard Petty's race car. On the nose and wing uprights was the rambunctious little bird with a racing helmet tucked under its right wing.

The Superbird's rear window was supported by two angled vertical stabilizers. The PLYMOUTH script on the quarter panel was done in the same font and size as on the side of Richard Petty's race car.

The roof extension needed to fit the

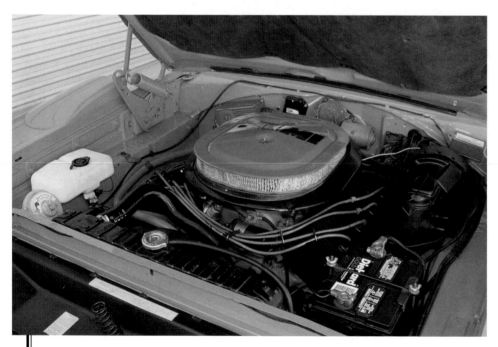

Only 135 Superbirds were powered by the Hemi engine. The rest of the 2,000 produced were equipped with a 440. Even though all other Hemi-equipped 1970 Road Runners were equipped with the Air Grabber hood, the Superbird was not. The distinctive Road Runner "Beep Beep" horn is at the left edge of the radiator tank. It's painted a shade of light purple and features the smirking face of the bird on a decal that states, "Voice of the Road Runner."

special rear window, which can be seen in the reflection off the driver's side C-pillar. Plymouth installed vinyl tops on all Superbirds to save the enormous amount of expensive metal finishing required to fit the rear window.

The Superbird's base engine was the 375-horsepower 440 Super Commando V-8, and the 425-horsepower street version of the 426 Hemi race engine was optional.

In 1970, the final year for the second-generation Dodge Charger, the Charger R/T had large rear-facing scoops added to the doors. The placement of the scoops required the relocation of the HEMI badges from the doors to the front fenders. *Dale Amy*

The 1971 Charger

In 1970 the Dodge Charger received only minor tweaks. Most notable were the redesigned grille and front bumper. The doors on the R/T received an added reversed scoop, which was located at the forward edge, covering the stamped depressions. Just as in the previous two years, the Hemi engine was available only in the R/T, and just 112 were sold.

In 1971, Dodge restyled the Charger and combined it with the Coronet. The new Charger/Coronet had to retain the aggressive good looks for the musclecar buyer, but also had to be sedate enough for the buyer of a four-door family car. Many enthusiasts believed that the new Charger had lost its individuality, because it shared a four-door platform.

The new Charger had a forward raked look that was attributed to the raised belt line. Although it had a two-inch-shorter wheelbase, the new Charger looked as long as the original. Many of the original Charger styling cues were still in place on the 1971 model. The grille was still rectangular in shape, surrounded by a halo bumper. Hidden headlights, previously standard on the Charger, were now optional on all but the base Charger. The basic Coke-bottle shape of the body was still there, along with the full wheel openings. The roof didn't have the tunneled rear window, but the deck lid retained a small spoiler.

High insurance surcharges took their toll on the sales of sleek Charger R/Ts in 1970, when only 10,337 were sold. Of that number, only 112 were equipped with the Hemi engine. *Dale Amy*

Hidden headlights, formerly standard on the Charger, were now optional. For 1971, the halo-style grille received a center bar. From the angle of this photograph, the Charger's Coke-bottle shape is apparent.

All 1971 Charger R/T models had a distinctive domed hood with flat black graphic and hood pins. All Hemi models had the trapdoor-style Ramcharger hood scoop.

The Charger R/Ts had special three-segment taillight lenses in an argent silver housing. The rear end treatment featured a contoured rear window that swept down to the deck lid and had a small built-in spoiler on the rear lip. This particular R/T also has an optional rear wing spoiler.

The 1971 Charger interiors were tastefully elegant. All R/Ts came with bucket seats covered in El Paso grained vinyl, and the gauges in front of the driver were nestled into a coved area of the instrument panel. The two larger dials housed the 150-mile-per-hour speedometer and 7,000-rpm tachometer.

In 1971 the Dodge Charger and Coronet were merged into one model. Unfortunately, this took away the uniqueness of the Charger, but it didn't diminish its visual appeal. The Charger's new sheet metal had an aggressive rake.

Bumblebee stripes, which had been common on previous Charger R/Ts, were no longer available in 1971. The new stripes, available only in black, wrapped around the cowl and swept down the belt line, terminating at the end of the quarter panel.

The 1971 Super Bee and Dodge R/T were both performance models, but of the two, the Super Bee was the plain vanilla model, having a more businesslike interior, offering fewer frills. The Super Bee's taillights are standard 1971 Charger units.

The R/T and the Super Bee

The R/T and Super Bee were performance models of the 1971 Charger. The R/T featured a domed and louvered hood with flat black accents. When the optional Hemi was ordered, the louvers were dropped in favor of a Ram Charger hood, also optional with the 440 engine. The R/T used unique door outer skins that had two vertical depressions at the door's leading edge. Inside these depressions were tape accents. The R/T also featured a body side stripe that started at the rear edge of the hood and swept along the belt line to the end of the quarter panel. The door accents and body side stripes, which came only in black, could be deleted. Small R/T emblems were added to the sides of the front fenders and to the rear edge of the deck lid. The Charger R/T had a special taillight lens that was divided into three sections per side. In 1971, there were only 63 Dodge Charger R/Ts sold with the Hemi engine.

The Super Bee was the inexpensive hot rod of the Charger lineup, and it came standard with a 300 horsepower 383 with options of a 440 or Hemi. Heavy-duty suspension, wide oval tires, and Rallye wheels were some of the hot standard equipment. Unlike the R/T, the Super Bee was fitted with the standard two-light-per-side Charger taillights. A special Super Bee hood decal was applied to the raised hood dome. The same body stripes ran from the cowl rearward on the R/T. Super Bee emblems were on the side of the front fender and on the back of the deck lid. Only 22 1971 Super Bees were equipped with Hemi engines.

The Superbird's base engine was the 375-horsepower 440 Super Commando V-8, and the 425-horsepower street version of the 426 Hemi race engine was optional.

In 1971, the Coronet was no longer available, and the Super Bee option was only available on the Charger. The Super Bee shared the R/T's domed hood (with Super Bee graphics) and body stripes. When equipped with a Hemi engine, the script on the side of the hood declared 426 HEMI.

Dual exhausts were standard on the Super Bee, but the rear wing was optional along with the small vertical bumper guards. Documentation showed that this particular 1971 Super Bee was originally delivered from Grand Spaulding Dodge. The owner has taken the time to add the proper Grand Spaulding license plate frame and decal to the deck lid—both status symbols in their day.

Chrysler's Pocket Rockets

To compete against the Mustang and soon-to-be-introduced Camaro, Chrysler's designers had to offer more than one body style. They also had to make room for larger engines. In the fall of 1966, Plymouth introduced its all-new Barracuda. In addition to the fastback, a coupe and a convertible were added to the lineup. The new Barracuda was longer, wider, and lower than the previous model. It had a muscular look and an engine lineup to match. With the availability of the 383-ci engine, it was the performance equal of Mustangs powered with the 390-ci engine. The 383 was only available with a four-speed manual or TorqueFlite transmission. Even with the two-inch-wider engine compartment, the 383 was a tight fit, and the accessory drive had to be redesigned. The new Barracuda sheet metal was fitted over the original platform, limiting the space available for a larger engine. Even when the Barracuda was reskinned in 1968, the engine compartment was limited to the 383. The only exceptions were the purpose-built drag race Hemi Barracudas.

The 1970 'Cuda and Challenger

In 1967, the musclecar boom experienced a sharp incline. At that time Chrysler's Advanced Styling Studios began work on what would eventually become the 1970 Barracuda. They worked in concert with the engineering groups to design a car with an engine compartment large enough to accommodate a 440 with air conditioning or a Hemi. In the musclecar wars, there was no substitute for cubic inches, and Chrysler was determined to build the most potent pony car ever.

To build such a car, an entirely new platform had to be created—the E-body. The larger B-body (Coronet/Charger) cowl was used as the starting point. The front sub frame and rear axle were also borrowed. (It is interesting to note that Camaro was constructed from Nova components in Chevy's parts bins.) The Advanced Styling group packaged the vehicle, determining wheelbase, seating positions, greenhouse, and door sills. With those parameters approved, the package was given to the Plymouth styling group. It was at this time that Chrysler management decided to build a Dodge equivalent—the Challenger. The Challenger would be positioned in the market as the upscale model to compete against the Mercury Cougar and Pontiac Firebird. While appearing similar to the Barracuda, the Challenger would be quite different.

Performance cars were made to be driven, and driving a Hemi 'Cuda is a definite adrenaline rush.

Both cars shared the upper body and the basic design theme of the long, low front end and an aggressive short, kicked-up rear deck. Only two body styles were to be built, a notch-back coupe and a convertible. A fastback wasn't in the cards. The Challenger's wheelbase was 110 inches, 2 inches longer than the Barracuda. The height was just a fraction over 50 inches, 2 inches lower than the previous Barracuda. Both cars, however, were low and wide. The new Barracuda's width was 74.7 inches, an increase of 5 inches over the previous model. The Challenger was even wider, at 76.1 inches. This width gave the E-bodied cars an exceptionally aggressive look from the front or rear. This look was accentuated with the addition of the fat 60-series Polyglas tires. When equipped with narrower standard tires, the E-bodies

Fat, 60-series tires were standard on the 'Cuda. They complemented the vehicle's overall low and wide design. This 1970 Hemi 'Cuda features the optional Elastomeric bumper and vinyl top.

The 1970 Dodge Challenger was built on the same E-body platform as the 'Cuda. While similar in appearance to the 'Cuda, its body was unique and rode on a slightly longer wheelbase.

The 1970 'Cuda was an entirely new vehicle and was designated as an E-body car. It was styled to compete against the hot-selling Mustangs and Camaros. It featured the long-nose short-deck design philosophy of its contemporaries.

The 1970 'Cudas and Challengers were only available in two-door hardtop (often called a notch back) and convertible body styles. The new E-bodies were two inches lower and five inches wider than the 1969 models.

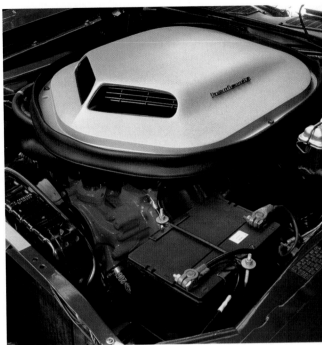

The sleek new E-bodies carried all the latest design trends, which included flush door handles, streamlined racing style mirrors, and hidden windshield wipers. Protruding through the hood on all Hemi-powered 'Cudas was the Shaker hood scoop.

All 1970 Hemi 'Cudas came equipped with the Shaker hood scoop. The opening to the carburetors was controlled by a lever under the instrument panel. A large rubber seal attached to the scoop sealed the hood, preventing water from entering the engine compartment.

The 'Cuda was the performance-oriented model of the 1970 Barracuda line, featuring a standard dual-scooped hood, hood pins, driving lights, and a rear taillight panel painted flat black.

All 1970 Hemi 'Cudas came with 15x7 Rallye wheels, extra heavy-duty suspension with special front torsion bars, a large front sway bar, unique heavy-duty rear leaf springs, and a Dana 60 rear axle.

Optional on the 1970 'Cuda were "hockey stick" stripes. These stripes accented the rear quarter panel, terminating with the engine's cubic-inch displacement near the taillight. When a 'Cuda was equipped with a Hemi, the stripes simply spelled out HEMI.

looked sadly out of proportion. The Challenger was longer at 191.3 inches compared to the Barracuda's 186.7 inches. Both cars offered full wheel openings, with the Challenger's more elliptical in shape than the Barracuda's. The Barracuda carried a soft horizontal character line down the side. The Challenger's body character line was more pronounced and it rose up over the rear wheel opening. It also flared out slightly, which can be attributed to the Challenger's dimensionally wider girth. The sides of both bodies tucked under severely in an area called "tumble home" by body designers. Both cars had flush door handles, hidden wipers, and ventless door glass—all the latest design trends coming out of the Detroit studios. The Challenger, true to its upscale image, had more bright trim, including thin wheel-opening moldings.

The front and rear of the new Challenger and Barracuda were also unique. Both were clean and classy designs. The Barracuda's oval-shaped grille had a single center peak accentuated by a series of deep-set horizontal bars. A pair of headlights was located at the outboard ends. The rolled-under valance panel below the thin horizontal bumper was painted body color, with an elliptical center opening allowing fresh air to the radiator. The

Challenger also had a thin horizontal bumper. Below the bumper, the opening in the body color valance panel was more rectangular. The deep-set mesh grille was accentuated with a thin rectangular chrome molding. Two quad headlights were at the outboard ends. The parking lights on the Barracuda were neatly blended into the upper portion of the grille, whereas the Challenger's circular parking lights were tunneled into the valance panel.

The Plymouth designers wanted a full urethane front end for the new Barracuda, similar to the '68 GTO, but unfortunately, the money wasn't available. What they were able to develop was the Elastomeric bumper option. This was an unchromed bumper with high-density urethane foam molded over the surface. It was then painted body color. The Elastomeric was available for both front or rear, giving the designers their body-color bumpers. This option was only available on the Barracuda.

The rear bumpers on the Barracuda and Challenger were thin horizontal bars with an upturn at each end. Small vertical bumper guards were located near the outboard ends and extended down from the bumper onto the rear valance panel. Depending on the engine option, dual exhaust outlets were carved into the rear valance panel on both cars.

The taillight treatment also differed on both E-body cars. The Barracuda had a flat inset panel that housed the license plate in the center and the taillights at the outboard ends. Each rear light fixture incorporated a backup light and had a pair of thin horizontal bars across the lenses. Because of the license plate location, the Barracuda's deck lid lock was offset to the right.

The Challenger's thin recessed taillight fixture carried the full width of the rear panel and featured a backup light in the center. The position of this light required the license plate to be mounted on the lower valance panel.

The Series

Both the Barracuda and Challenger could be ordered in three series. The Barracuda was the base model, followed by the Gran Coupe, and then the sporty 'Cuda. The Challenger also had three series: the base Challenger, the optional SE series, and the R/T (Road and Track).

The 'Cuda was easily identified by its special twin-scoop hood, hood pins, driving lights, Rallye wheels, and flat black taillight panel. An optional "hockey stick" body stripe was available. It slashed along the quarter panel, terminating with the engine's displacement figures in prominent letters or, on the cars equipped with the Hemi engine, the word HEMI.

Chrysler's designers were not restricted to adding a new body to an old platform when creating the new E-body 'Cuda. The 'Cuda's body sides carried a smart horizontal character line and a small lip on the full wheel openings. The 'Cuda's tightly integrated design can be seen in the way the rear valance panel was designed to blend smoothly into the vertical bumper guard.

The Dodge R/T came with a standard power bulge hood that featured twin inlets and hood pins. This hood was available with a special blackout paint treatment. Like the 'Cuda, the R/T also featured white letter tires on Rallye wheels. As part of the R/T package, a rear Bumblebee stripe or full-length body stripe was offered at no cost. The body side stripe accented the Challenger's side character line. The Bumblebee stripe had the effect of chopping off the rear of the car.

When ordered with the Hemi engine, the 'Cuda came standard with the Shaker hood scoop (it was optional on 'Cudas equipped with a 340, 383, or 440 engine). This

Bold colors were the norm for the early 1970s, and Plymouth pleased its customers with a long list of vivid colors that included Vitamin C, Lemon Twist, and this shade is called TorRed.

scoop protruded through the hood and, as advertised, shook and shimmied while the engine revved. It had two openings in the front that allowed fresh air to enter the carbs when a lever on the instrument panel opened a valve in the scoop. Interestingly, the Shaker hood scoop was also optional on the Challenger with the Hemi engine. On both the 'Cuda and Challenger, the Shaker hood could be ordered in argent silver, flat black, or body color. The cold air flowing through the scoop enhanced engine performance by a few horsepower. But the visual impact was just as important as the horsepower, especially when everyone was able to see the word HEMI on the side of the scoop.

Colors, Interiors and Options

The catalog of colors for the Barracuda and Challenger was long and kaleidoscopic. Chrysler targeted these cars for the youth market and wanted the colors to be as bright and brazen as the cars themselves. Some of the more catchy colors were TorRed, Lemon Twist, Vitamin C, Sublime, Lime Light, Go-Mango, and of course, Hemi Orange. With the combinations of body styles and series, the addition of body stripes, hood

configurations, and tire and wheel combinations, no two cars looked alike.

The interiors of the Barracuda and Challenger were simple but not as well executed as the exterior styling.

The 'Cuda's interior featured vinyl-covered high-back bucket seats. Leather seats (as pictured) were an option. This 'Cuda's interior also features an optional three-spoke steering wheel, center console, and "Pistol Grip" shifter.

The parking lights were integrated into the upper grille opening. The deep-set black grille was accented by a single thin horizontal red stripe. Instead of chrome, body-colored Elastomeric bumpers could be specified for the front and rear of the 1970 'Cuda. The small circular driving light below the bumper was standard as part of the 'Cuda package.

The offset trunk-lock cylinder is partially hidden by the 'Cuda nameplate. The lock was placed there because rear design did not permit a center-mounted lock. All 'Cudas featured dual exhaust with bright rectangular tips that extended through the rear valance panel.

An excess of plastic tended to make the interior look cheap when compared to competitive models, such as the Camaro and Mustang. Typical of the pony cars of the era, the Barracuda and Challenger had front bucket seats and small rear bench seats. The door and quarter trim panels were molded with an integral armrest. In front of the driver, the padded instrument panel was coved. The three-spoked steering wheel sat high in relation to the driver's seat. This elicited complaints from journalists when first test driving the Barracuda and Challenger.

When the Mustang was introduced in 1964, it was offered with a wealth of options, so the buyer could build the car of his or her dreams. When the Camaro was released, Chevrolet followed the same philosophy, offering a large number of possible option combinations. Chrysler followed suit with the Barracuda and Challenger. The wide array of interior and exterior options included leather seats, center console, Rallye wheels, rear window louvers, vinyl roof, and even a vacuum-operated trunk release.

These options continued under the hood. A host of different engines were offered for the Barracuda and Challenger, culminating with the Hemi. At a cost of $1,227, the Hemi option added considerably to the $2,800 base price for each car. When adding the Hemi, many heavy-duty components were included, so the car could keep up with the engine. Only two transmissions were offered with the Hemi option, the TorqueFlite automatic and a four-speed manual. Selecting the gears on the four-speed was done with a Hurst shifter. This shifter didn't use a ball or T-handle; instead it used a vertical shift handle initially called a "strip-grip" shifter, which later became known as the "pistol grip" shifter. Barracudas and Challengers with a 440 or a Hemi were equipped with extra heavy-duty front torsion bars and a large-diameter (0.94) front stabilizer bar. The rear suspension had an unusual combination of leaf springs. The left side had five full leafs with two half leafs and the right side had six full leafs. Hemi cars were not equipped with a rear stabilizer bar. The Hemi-powered Barracudas and Challengers all came with the heavy-duty Dana rear axle that rode on 15x7-inch wheels mounting F60X15 tires.

The 1970 E-body Dodge Challenger had a pronounced horizontal character line along the side that rose up over the rear wheel opening. The Challenger's R/T option provided the same level of standard performance options as the 'Cuda.

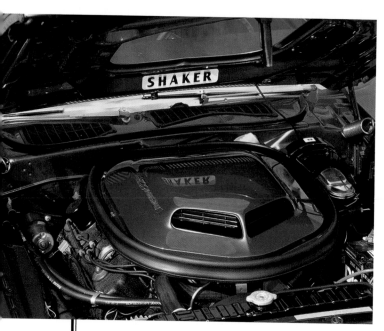

The big Hemi engine fits snugly into the E-body engine compartment. This Hemi Challenger R/T is equipped with the optional Shaker hood scoop. The Shaker hood scoops were available in flat black, argent silver, or body color. The chrome emblem on the side of the scoop proudly announces that the engine below is a 426 HEMI.

Fast Cars and Hot Sales

Motor Trend magazine writer Bill Sanders tested a new 1970 Hemi 'Cuda for the September 1969 issue. In his words, the new Hemi 'Cuda was "quite impressive." He wrote, "With the new Hemi 'Cuda a quarter-mile goes by so fast you hardly know you started. Even though our car had the widest optional F60X15 tires, we still experienced considerable wheel spin, which cut e.t.s. With a 4:10:1 axle ratio, all acceleration figures were out of sight, naturally. Plymouth's own version of the 'Shaker' hood adds to total performance." The Hemi 'Cuda Sanders drove was equipped with a TorqueFlite transmission, power steering, and power brakes, and it tripped the quarter-mile clocks in 13.7 seconds at a speed of 101.2 miles per hour.

Selling 666 units, the 1970 Hemi 'Cudas commanded the second-highest production numbers for any individual model Hemi-powered Chrysler product (the 1968 Road Runner is first). Of that total, 14 were convertibles. In 1970, 356 Hemi Challengers were produced; only nine were convertibles. The 1970 Challenger also accomplished its mission of outselling the Mercury Cougar. In total, the Challenger sold more than 76,000 units compared to the Cougar's 72,000.

The 1971 Models

For 1971, only minor but distinctive changes were made to the Barracudas and Challengers. The Barracuda's grille was restyled by adding four additional vertical bars. This new grille is commonly called a "cheese grater" by collectors because of its similarity to the kitchen appliance. The two large headlights were replaced with a quad headlight arrangement similar to the Challenger's. The grille was either painted argent silver or body color. Barracudas with chrome bumpers received the argent grille, and those equipped with the Elastomeric bumpers received a body color grille. Four nonfunctional louvers were added to the sides of the front fenders. These louvers are commonly called "gills" for obvious reasons. Thin chrome wheel opening moldings were added, and the taillights were slightly revised. If you had a high-performance engine in your 1971 'Cuda, why not advertise it to the world with Billboard stripes? These stripes replaced the hockey stick stripes. They were enormous, covering most of the quarter panel and half of the door. In foot-high letters on the leading edge, the billboard announced to the world the cubic-inch displacement of the high-performance V-8 under the hood or, in the case of the Hemi, displayed those four famous letters HEMI.

The 1971 Challenger grille also received a minor change. The full-width inset chrome rectangle was split in the center into two smaller rectangles. In the rear, the full-width taillight was split into two and the center backup light was integrated into the lens on each side. The R/T hardtop received a new set of wider body side stripes that terminated at the C-pillar. For 1971 the R/T convertible was discontinued.

1971 Plymouth 'Cuda

When the Barracuda debuted in mid-1964, it was anything but a musclecar. But in true Ugly Duckling style, the Barracuda grew to become the envy of the musclecar market. Each year, Plymouth refined the Barracuda, transforming it from a Corvair- and Falcon-fighter to a fearsome Mustang- and Camaro-killer.

At no time was the 'Cuda—introduced in 1969 as a separate performance-oriented version of the Barracuda—more refined than 1971. When Plymouth first unleashed the 'Cuda option, it did so to address power shortcomings in the aging fastback Barracuda. In 1970, the Barracuda lineup was redesigned with a Camaro-esque long hood/short deck body that rippled with muscle.

For 1971, the one-year-old body was updated to smooth the design's few rough edges. Under the hood,

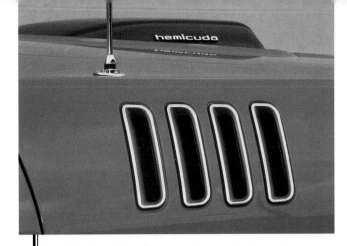

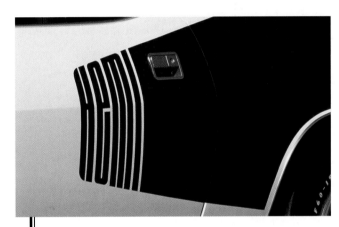

Added to the front fenders of the 1971 'Cudas were "gills," which were four nonfunctional louvers.

In 1971, Billboard stripes replaced the hockey sticks. Throughout the era of the street Hemi, this was the most pronounced and extravagant display of engine size.

At a cost of close to $5,000, a new 1971 Hemi 'Cuda was not inexpensive in its day. Today, it would take almost 10 times that amount to buy one of the few produced.

All 1971 Hemi 'Cudas came standard with F60x15 tires on 15x7 steel rims. Rallye rims, standard on all 1970 'Cudas, were optional in 1971.

the 'Cuda engine lineup was warmed-over from 1970 and most engines were re-rated to reflect the auto industry's move to the Society of Automotive Engineers (SAE) net horsepower ratings—which more realistically indicated how much power an engine would produce as installed in a production vehicle, rather than on an engine dynamometer. (Of course, any deliberate horsepower understatements by manufacturers in previous years still make comparisons tricky.) Otherwise, the 340, 383, both the four-barrel and six-barrel 440s, and the legendary Hemi were unchanged. GM and Ford made quick and drastic changes in their 1971

performance engine lineups, making the 'Cudas appear all the more awesome.

Thanks to the chassis and suspension systems introduced in 1970, the 'Cuda continued to be one of the best-handling cars on the market, especially when equipped with the lightweight but plenty powerful 340 small-block engine, which produced a re-rated and still underrated 235 horsepower in 1971. Naturally, the straightline crowd was more attracted to the 440s and Hemis, but at $884 (plus the cost of the mandatory four-speed and other heavy-duty options) the elephant motor was a stretch for all but a lucky 115 'Cuda buyers—just 7 of whom went for their Hemi in a convertible body.

As exciting and powerful as the 1971 'Cuda was, there was still one area in which it couldn't compete with Camaros and Mustangs: sales. Those models sold more than 100,000 units each, whereas the entire Barracuda line didn't even account for 19,000 registrations that year—and just 6,602 were 'Cudas.

The Hemi was the ultimate Barracuda engine, but a variety of performance engines were available including the 335-horsepower 383 and the 390-horsepower 440 Wedge motors for the cost-conscious. A high-revving, triple two-barrel, 290-horsepower 340 was available in the AAR 'Cuda, which was Dodge's homologation special for Trans-Am road racing.

The short deck and long hood emulated the Mustang and Camaro, but the clean lines and distinctive styling were all Mopar. The 'Cuda featured a blacked-out taillamp panel and was available with a deck lid wing and rear window slats.

The following year, Chrysler detuned its musclecar program. The 'Cuda engine lineup was gutted. The only "performance" engine kept on the option list was the 340, which picked up 5 horsepower on paper but was obviously far less powerful than the lower-rated 340 of 1971.

For the brief span of one model year, the 1971 'Cuda was the pinnacle of Chrysler musclecar creation, and for many today, the ultimate muscle-car ever.

The Barracuda was first released in 1964, but the 1970 E-Body Barracuda joined the upper echelon of musclecars and was a genuine challenger to the Camaro and Mustang. With the exception of the Dart, the Barracuda was the lightest and smallest Mopar musclecar in 1970. When equipped with a Hemi, it became the fastest Mopar.

Index